Published by BurmanBooks
260 Queens Quay West
Suite 1102
Toronto, Ontario
Canada M5J 2N3

Cover design: Nancy Newman
Photo of Author: Yanka and Henk Van der Kolk
Background Photo: iStock Images by Mammuth
Interior design: Lara Vanderheide
Editing: Anna Watson

Distribution:
NewLeaf Distribution
401 Thorton Rd.
Lithia Springs, GA 30122-1557
ISBN: 978-1-927005-38-5
Printed and bound in The United States of America

DEDICATION

For Colleen

Your loving heart was a beacon of light
as I wandered through the shadows.
I found my way, now healed, soul free
forever grateful as my worth grows.

ACKNOWLEDGMENTS

I am blessed to feel the presence of my parents, Tom and Margaret, who continue to help me from heaven. I sense them every day showing me the way to the answers that I always seem to be seeking. To all eight siblings, Tim, Peter, Tom, Marcy, Matthew, P.J., Andy and Pat who have helped me learn so much about relationships in this life and what it is to be a small part of a large family.

I will always be grateful to my publisher, Sanjay Burman who recognized my soul across a room, knew that I had a book in me ready to be written and for providing me with the awesome opportunity to do so.

To everyone who has ever asked me for help through Coaching, Hypnosis, Angel readings or spiritual advice, I thank you. You have helped me practice my gifts and recognize the lesson in it for me. Everyone I encounter during my day, my colleagues and friends who have ever laughed with me and at my jokes, I thank you for getting it and getting me.

To every student who has ever found their way into my classroom and every student who ever will. I'm only sent the best and you are the best part of my day as I laugh with you, learn from you and revel in your light. We find each other again in each lifetime and it`s good to know you once more.

I feel grateful for the heavenly presence of so many angels and guides that are around me always helping me as I channel their messages from heaven. Thanks God, for lending them to me.

TABLE OF CONTENTS

1. listen

Our bodies communicate to us clearly and specifically, if we are willing to listen to them.

-Shakti Gawain

We're all on a journey; some of realize it and some of us don't.

The only journey I had ever been aware of in my life was the journey by foot taken from my apartment to the beer store when I was in university and without a car. It was quite a distance but I was always up for it because of the benefits once I arrived home again.

Sometimes asking for help is the beginning of a journey. Maybe that's when mine really started. When I realized that I was having trouble with my health, I started to look at where I had been in life and where I was going.

What does perfect health really look like, anyway? We all talk about it, but what is it? I think that if you were to ask ten people, you would probably get ten different responses. What if you were born sick but never diagnosed with any illness? You wouldn't have any reference from which to measure excellent health, great health, good health or bad health.

That, I know now, has been my experience. All I knew was the way I had always felt, so I thought that was normal.

For twelve years, I had been a teacher; a challenging, intense career in which I'd interact with hundreds of people in a variety of relationships all day long. At the end of my school day, I'd go to the gym to work out, then go home, cook and eat dinner and then attempt to fit in some creative endeavour to help soothe my artistic soul; I'm also an artist and need to create. At the time, I ran a small art and design business part-time too on a freelance basis along with working at my full-time job as an educator.

Although I was always high energy, full of craziness and often the life of the party, I would use up all my energy when I was out, spending it and then collapsing later at home, having nothing left for me; no balance. The medical professionals I consulted could not decipher my health issues.

For many years I had searched out doctors, telling them of my symptoms, but always got the same response – I worked too hard and should take every Wednesday or Friday off. As if. Wouldn't employees everywhere want a shorter work week? The Board of Education that I was working for would not have appreciated that idea. I would listen to them, and then simply go back to my daily routine of running to school, running at school, running away from school and running after school – but what was I really running from? And what was I running to? For a long time, I bought into that doctor's suggestion that I was in good health, just working too hard and that everything was essentially fine with me.

But something in me knew that wasn't the case. I needed to find out why I felt like I was boiling wool in my gut, was bloated and often had difficulty digesting food properly. I felt anxious, stressed and lethargic. I had hypoglycaemia and suffered from extreme fatigue yet I was often unable to sleep well. I had circulatory problems that manifested in Reynaud's disease, a condition where the blood flow drains from one or more fingers when it's cold or when I was stressed out.

The worst for me, though, were the cognitive problems like memory loss, brain fog and mental confusion. I was unable to get through a sentence and remember what I was talking about. I was unable to go to the phone book, look up a number, put the book away while repeating the number in my head and arrive at the phone and make the call. Inevitably, I would forget the number and have to look it up again and write it down. How did I function while trying to teach is the question? And every day I pushed myself to show up, be professional and present myself in the best way I knew how. To keep pushing through the discomfort became a habit and something that I took for granted. I thought that was normal; be strong, keep going.

Every six months to a year later, I would try to find a new or different doctor to explain my symptoms to. Those doctors were never able to see that all of these symptoms belonged to an illness, call it something and then give me direction as to how to proceed with healing and feeling better. I was depending on the medical profession to have all the answers when I see now that it has been part of my journey to learn to take responsibility for my own health and find my own answers.

I saw that something was calling me deeper and this lack of ease in my body was in fact screaming at me. But I was so toxic and brain-fogged that it made it difficult to listen, hear or understand that all these symptoms had a message for me.

If I decided to go away for some rest at March Break for example, I would be so exhausted all I could do was just lie in the sun for a week. I would position myself close to the bar and I'd move from the sun to the beer and back to the sun again. Who needed to eat? That took too much energy. And God forbid my travelling companion should ever suggest we go on a day long excursion somewhere for fun. No way riding a donkey through a tropical forest to observe tree frogs mating appealed to me. That took too much energy. Although, I did notice that while lying in the sun, I'd open my eyes periodically to witness everything around me mating; must have been the heat. The birds were screwing in the trees so I'd turn over. The salamanders were humping each other under my chaise. The ants were even fornicating in the grass. I guess I didn't mind watching the sex....I just didn't want to travel a distance to see it. That took too much energy.

I didn't know I could listen to my body and I didn't know that I should listen. I was not aware then that symptoms are the body's way of speaking to us to tell us what it needs in order to be healthy. Our body's natural state is to be healthy so it is always working to get back to this optimal place. Sometimes my body has spoken to me with a message through pain which finally got my attention because it is difficult to ignore pain. I know now, many years later, after going through a Life Coaching program with Colleen Hoffman-Smith and reading her book, *Pocket Guide to Your Heart*, (Heart Bridge Publishing, 2003,) that underneath any illness, there sits a negative emotion. We hold these unfelt emotions inside us and they can eventually manifest as an illness in the body.

The notion that we create our own disease was something I was introduced to through Macrobiotics which has its roots in Traditional Chinese Medicine. I was intrigued. How could we be the creator of our cancers, colds and broken limbs? At the time, I was unable to see how this was the truth for me, but I was open to investigating the idea further. Perhaps it was really my curiosity and my desire to learn about this theory that drew me to find out more about it. I feel strongly now, many years later, that we heal ourselves and that doctors help facilitate that healing by working along with us. As I learned later in my journey, we are spiritual beings and in this lifetime we are learning to live in a physical body. Listening to it is part of that learning. It is necessary for us to not control or impose our will on our body but rather listen with a gentleness and love that will allow us to take care of it the best way possible for optimal health.

But I didn't start out knowing those truths. Like most other people in our society, I felt pressed for time and was looking for an easy way out.

It would have taken too much energy to make my own lunch and take it to school every day, so I ate the cafeteria's Special of the Day. Even if the fish had winter coats on (others called it batter), or the chilli had lost its individuality because the beans were cooked so long that they all smooshed into one big conglomerate, it was ready and waiting. Cafeteria food was processed, refined, deep-fried and fast.

I did not know it at the time, but it was the worst thing for me. However, I did eventually come to see that what I ate at lunch was affecting me in a negative way because after lunch, I would return to my office and crash. It was impossible for me to stay awake and I would literally pass out at my desk as my body reacted to something I had eaten.

How do you feel after you eat? Do you ever experience symptoms of fatigue or pain? You too, may be eating something that is not good for your body or your health. You know what it is because your body is telling you, so listen.

At the end of the school day I was also faced with another challenge when the drive home along the highway involved traffic congestion which slowed the car down as I too slowed down and my body crashed again. I would fight to stay awake.

Did You Know?
Between three and five o'clock nearly everyone is hypoglycaemic – which means that you have low blood sugar and this manifests in bodily fatigue. This is because we have not eaten since lunch, so I usually have a healthy snack to help keep me alert and awake.

Do you ever feel drowsy at that time of day? Eating a few almonds or another source of protein will help you feel better as it enters your system. Feeling more relaxed after eating a snack then is also a benefit because hypoglycaemia creates anxiety in the body.

One day at school, while I was enjoying a plate of French fries and gravy, a colleague handed me a book about Candida Albicans and I found direction, help, support and answers in it. It was the first time I had ever heard of such an illness so with the information this lead provided I was able to diagnose myself with this disorder.

Candida is a common genus of fungus, a yeast which can come into a state of overgrowth in the body and its growth is fed by sugar which the body craves. Candida overgrowth creates great toxicity which is painful as your body is actually in the process of being poisoned. Food allergies and viruses are also created which help to break down the immune system even further.

Taking antibiotics is one of the culprits because they destroy the bad bacteria that is making us sick but are indiscriminate and eat the good bacteria as well, which is something that we need to keep our body in balance, healthy and strong. Seventy percent of our immune system is in our gut and if I had known better I would have taken probiotics every day to help replenish the good flora and also help keep my immune system boosted and strong.

Are you making sure to have a strong immune system by taking supplements of Acidophilus (Lactobacillus acidophilus), a common bacteria that lives in our small intestine every morning on an empty stomach? It is also said to make B vitamins and vitamin K which are essential for good health.

I knew nothing of nutrition at the time and had a major craving for beer, bread, potatoes and pasta. The beer always won out and I drank a lot of it. I actually thought that craving was because I was of Irish descent and that it was just in my DNA; not true. I had several girlfriends who were watching their weight and were challenged by their cravings for sweet things. I never wanted to eat sweets but my sugar high came from drinking alcohol instead, always feeding the Candida's growth. Drinking beer for me was the same as my friends eating cake. It was all sugar. But I never had a bad time when I was drinking and I never got the same high from a cookie.

Because allopathic medicine and general practitioners had not been able to diagnose me for so long, I decided to go in the new direction of natural medicine. Dr. Carolyn Dean was a leading specialist in Candida Albicans and held both an allopathic degree along with also being a Naturopath. I learned a lot about health while working with her and it helped me when I realized that I couldn't just take a prescribed medicine to get rid of Candida, but rather had to work hard at changing the way I lived to heal. I really needed to slow down and learn how to take better care of myself.

Anyone who has ever had cancer has had an overgrowth of Candida. When I understood this truth from my doctor, I thought of my mother who had died from pancreatic cancer when my youngest brother was only six years old and knew that she too had Candida. I had taken antibiotics as a child, probably for minor things like dental work, stepping on a piece of glass and needing stitches or some infection a kid might get. The benefits of antibiotics are evident but if the good intestinal flora is never replenished after taking them, it can cause an imbalance which can affect the immune system. Many years ago, people with Candida overgrowth were often misdiagnosed and put into insane asylums because the toxic effects made them behave with what appeared to be mental health symptoms; depression, anxiety, erratic behaviour, emotional outbursts and memory loss.

It took more than one attempt for me to give up sugar as I committed to a Candida-free diet for six weeks. It was like kicking a cocaine or heroin addiction; not that I'd know what that was like but, it was intense. I wanted to run up and down the stairs banging my head against the walls from the desire and pain it created as my body screamed out for it. It was one of the most difficult things I have ever done. I had to gradually wean myself off sugar by getting rid of everything white, including all flours, corn, fruit, alcohol and wheat. To stop consuming these foods all at once was a challenge but I needed to do it because they are converted into sugar in the body. In doing this, I also tried to be kind to myself and not expect this new diet to be accomplished overnight, but that was a challenge too.

Many researchers believe that sugar is the basis of all disease in North America today and in William Dufty's book, *Sugar Blues*, (Grand Central Life & Style Publishing, 1986), he writes about how he gave up eating sugar, got rid of the pain and illness that he suffered and even looked fifteen years younger because of it.

How much sugar do you eat? Try to not think of sugar as just the white, refined substance you put in your coffee but also in the form of white flour, anything sweet and even white rice – all of these all sugars.

Do you need the sugar you are eating every day? We can live without it. Try to cut back on it and be aware of the differences you feel and the improvements you see in your body.

Very often, when women have a bout of Candida overgrowth, it will manifest itself in a yeast infection. This is uncomfortable with its burning and itching but the symptoms are telling us there is something out of balance within us. I had never had a yeast infection but the Candida in my body had flourished and was in my blood and bones, perhaps also due to the fact that the good intestinal flora was never put back into my gut. My mother did not know about probiotics and how important they were to have a healthy immune system, so it appears now that my intestinal flora and my immune system may have been out of balance my entire life.

After six weeks of staying away from any Candida-causing foods, there was not a bit of difference in how I felt. I knew that I had to persevere to feel like I was making progress. Again, I just needed to continue to learn how to take care of myself.

If you get a yeast infection, ask yourself if you are eating a well-balanced diet. If not, take care of yourself by staying away from any sweet, refined, flour-based and white foods or mouldy cheeses for a while until you feel your body back in balance and the yeast overgrowth is gone. Taking probiotics every day will boost your immune system as well as add good flora into your gut where you need it.

Ask yourself how hard you are working and take a look to see if you are pushing yourself too much every day. How much stress are you under? Remember to slow down and take care of yourself enough to heal a yeast overgrowth before it becomes something more serious because you haven't been listening. Men have Candida too; it's not just women.

I had a lactose intolerance test done to see if I had an allergy to dairy as it too, can cause many of the symptoms I was suffering from. The results were evident even before the test was completed when I was injected with lactose at half hour intervals to monitor my reaction. I began to crash immediately and fall asleep as it entered my system. The groggy, drugged feeling I experienced made me think of the way I had been reacting after I ate lunch every day and realized that the milk I was drinking was acting like poison in my body and that I had an allergy to it. My results did come back positive to lactose intolerance. I took all dairy out of my diet and this also helped improve the other symptoms like cramping and bloating that sometimes bothered me.

Do you feel any symptoms after you eat dairy? Maybe taking it out of your diet for six weeks is a good idea. After a period without it, slowly re-introducing it back into your diet can tell you if it is an appropriate choice for you or not. Your body will tell you if it produces any symptoms, so listen.

My doctor suggested that I have food allergy testing by Red Paw Data Services which employs a more natural, non-invasive technique called electro-dermal testing. A dull, brass rod is held in the hand, is connected to a computer and gives you immediate results. It can give you a list of foods to stay away from. I learned that cravings are often our body's way of getting us to eat foods that we are allergic to and should avoid but are dying to have. Understanding this has helped me because I became aware of my cravings and know that they too represent symptoms. I had this type of allergy testing done every six months for many years and it gave me clear direction as to my diet and what I should avoid. At first when I was very ill, the list of offending foods was really long. Later, it became shorter. Eventually, some of those foods I could eat again. Some I have never gotten back as an edible choice.

Be aware of any reaction you may experience after eating, any pain or discomfort and ask yourself if you would benefit from this kind of allergy testing. It's an excellent way to know what foods are appropriate to eat and it is another way to learn to listen to your body and take care of it.

When I was a teenager in high school, I was not allowed to stay home from school when I felt sick. My mother probably needed that time to herself to renew her energy with fewer children around for the day, but this training was probably the beginning of how I learned to act strong and ignore how I really felt. This would also have been the source of my ignoring what my body was telling me and learning not to listen when it told me what it needed. I was being taught to push through the pain and ignore the fact that I wasn't feeling well; to be strong and keep going.

We become what we are taught by our parents. I always admired how my father could get up in the morning and be ready to leave the house for work within 15 minutes. He never ate breakfast. That was not a healthy choice, but I took on the same behaviour for a long time because I thought then it was a good thing because dad did it.

Are you taking the time each day to fuel your body with meals, especially first thing in the morning? If you find yourself not eating because you are rushed, stop and realize that there is enough time in each day to do everything that you need to be healthy. Take responsibility by getting up a little earlier to be able to consume the food that creates the energy you will need for the day; eating healthily will help you be successful in life. You also will notice that you're more peaceful once you start your day this way. Take the time; it's important.

Along with a newfound emphasis on food, listening to symptoms and having testing, I decided to sign up for *The Relaxation Response,* (www.elibay.com) a course geared to Type A personalities. It teaches those of us who are prone to be workaholics how to relax and reduce stress in our lives using breathing and meditation techniques. The terms Type A and Type B personalities refer to a psychological theory which describe two different personality types in people, Type A being high strung, driven and more heart attack prone. Type B is much more easy-going and relaxed. At the time, I was definitely a Type A. The good news is that you can change your behaviour and become a Type B instead of a Type A, because I have done it.

I can remember clearly the first time we meditated at the end of class. Eli's soothing, calming voice gradually took me into theta state where brain activity slows almost to the point of sleep, but not quite. This is where we meditate from and where the magic happens. I felt myself leaving my body, free of any stress or worry, feeling the lightness of my soul. It was amazing for me to be able to hear and be aware of everything around me at the same time that I was in a trance. The only sound we would often hear during these meditation sessions was a classmate who went beyond theta state into REM (rapid eye movement) and began snoring as he crossed the line into sleep. The benefits of sleep, although restorative and healing, do not begin to compare to the benefits of meditation so the classmate who slept through the meditation sessions lost out.

The peace, relaxation and joy that are a result of meditation are something that I brought into my daily life as a practice. It is a powerful tool to deal with stress release and to listen for the answers to life's questions that we are all searching for. Some say that praying is talking to God, but that meditation is listening. Do you need help with handling stress in your life? Do you want to feel more joy and peace? Learn to meditate.

It also helped a lot in my job as I learned to focus on my work and stay present when things became chaotic around me. My colleagues would be anxious and complain when we were hit with an unexpected deadline or some pressure to have exams marked in a specific time, but I was able to stay outside the storm and remain calm. I saw the difference that meditation made in my behaviour almost immediately and my colleagues did as well and commented on it.

Would you benefit from knowing how to not get caught up in the chaos that sometimes surrounds us all? Do you feel joy every day? Meditation helps us to feel blissful, positive thoughts and deal with the creative problem solving necessary for us to get through each day.

LISTEN TO YOUR BODY EXERCISE

Here is an exercise that you can practice, where you listen to your body and it tells you what it needs. It is a simple, effective tool.

- Sit down in a comfortable chair somewhere, close your eyes and put your hands on your lap and your feet on the floor.
- Take a few deep, slow breaths calming yourself as you count down from three to one.
- Say silently inside your body to yourself, ¨Body, what do you need¨? Then, listen for the answer.
- You may receive it in one word or it may be a feeling, but you will get an answer. The answer could be anything from

food, rest, water, to fun or help.

- If you don't get an answer right away, just ask your body again. If the answer does not come to you immediately, it could come later on, so don't give up, just keep listening.
- Don't try too hard because you could be blocking yourself from hearing the answers. Just believe, relax, ask and listen.
- Then, give your body what it needs. Practicing this exercise will help you listen and it will become easier the more you do it.

Our bodies talk to us through the symptoms we have, so be conscious of them and listen to what they are telling you. I know that I am here as a spiritual being, learning how to live in my physical body and when I am working with it and listening to it tell me what it needs, I benefit with great health.

As I learned to treat my body with care, listen, eat healthy, rest and slow down when necessary, I began to see positive results in my life. Meditating to learn to get back to the peace that is within each of us is as important as is asking for help from doctors when we need it and listening to our bodies when we feel that something is out of order inside us.

Keep searching for the answers. They are within you; just listen.

2. change

If there is not struggle, there is no progress.

-Frederick Douglass

In less than a year, I had changed every aspect of my lifestyle; I had to. My energy level really did not allow me to be social or spend time with friends, and I was often left feeling overwhelmed at even the suggestion of a party. I had committed to stay on a clean, healthy diet with no sugars, nothing refined and no alcohol; everything you might find at a social gathering. I was about to learn however, that it was going to take a lot more than just making a decision in my head to affect such radical lifestyle change.

The world now seemed to have many temptations that could keep me from my commitment to perfect health and I often felt vulnerable in situations where I used to be able to drink and eat anything I wanted. When I did venture out to a party, I would take my own food and did not drink but when everyone else was partying, it resulted in me feeling left out.

When I thought about it, I realized that this feeling actually went back to my childhood and being one of nine siblings. Because my sister and I were two girls with seven brothers, my father often would take the boys on excursions or to movies as an opportunity to be together as boys and bond. This could have been one of the times when I first felt left out as I remember feeling like it didn't seem fair that because they were boys they got to spend time with my father and I was left at home.

This became easier for me once I later learned that all negative emotions felt as an adult really come from triggering the memory of a childhood experience in disappointment. Learning to get to that underlying hurt is essential when I am working on healing my wounds.

In order to address this part of me that did not feel good enough to be included, it was necessary to feel that pain rather than staying away from that uncomfortable feeling by pushing it inside, where it sits in muscles or organs and festers. I am with it by bringing it to the surface, to a conscious level to feel it and heal.

Being alone with myself as an adult, I talked to my father out loud and told him how I felt and how disappointed I was to be left behind. In doing this, I feel and heal this pain by screaming or crying if I need to when the childhood hurt comes up. Through this exercise, I release that old emotion from my body and feel lighter and better as a result. I also know now that doing this one time may not heal it entirely and this old hurt might resurface again in a triggered reaction to something else in my life. When and if it continues to happen, I just allow myself to use that feeling, to do my work and further heal that wound within me. I have learned to be self-aware as I recognize when I am triggered in that way and now can deal with the underlying truth.

Are you ever triggered by someone in your life and feel emotional pain like anger, guilt or sadness? Is there someone who you are always triggered by? If so, they are really a gift because it is an opportunity to use that triggered emotion to heal your wound by taking responsibility for it; don't blame someone else for your emotional reaction. When this happens, try to be with any negative feelings and not push them away. Just experience the emotion and react to it as you feel compelled to.

Try to also be mindful of any childhood experiences that could mirror what you are reacting to as an adult. Can you take better care of yourself each day by spending some time remembering and feeling those old, unfelt emotions? This will help you as an adult to get to the source of that trigger which is your pain. Feel it; it helps heal the wound.

I love Louise Hay's, *You Can Heal Your Life* (Hay House Publishing, 1987,) which has become a wonderful resource. She talks about working on yourself and learning to recognize that we are individually all responsible for our experiences. Louise Hay teaches that releasing resentment will even heal cancer and that self-acceptance and self-approval is what we all need to be healthy and happy. She has compiled a list of physical issues and explains what unfelt emotion is beneath them and what each part of our body represents in terms of these emotions. If I am unsure about some area of my body that shows me a symptom, her book helps me zero in on the emotional truth that is at the basis of the symptom so I can take responsibility for it and work on healing it.

Do you have symptoms and are unsure of why they are manifesting in a specific body part? For example, anything to do with legs reminds me that I hold understanding in them so I ask myself what is it that I am not understanding in some area of my life when I experience a leg symptom. Then I take responsibility for it, and feel it. The symptom will disappear once I have healed the emotional source of it. Try this because it will work for you too.

When I was beginning my journey to healing, I didn't know it but everyone who takes drugs or drinks alcohol is trying to numb themselves in order to avoid feeling something they are uncomfortable with. These feelings can be anger, sadness, guilt, loneliness and more. So many events in our society are celebrated with alcohol and it took me a long time to not miss it once I decided to abstain. It was like saying good-bye to an old friend; perhaps an old friend who kept me from feeling something. I knew that at least for a while I would have to isolate myself and spend more time alone, going inside to heal so I stopped socializing with family and friends. It was easy at times though because the notion of going out to an event was too much for me; I was feeling so weak.

Truthfully, I also needed to spend time alone to de-stress through meditation so that I could listen for the spiritual direction that I intuitively believed was coming to me. This could only be done if I was not numbing my emotions; I needed to have a clear sense of what I was feeling. At the time I was unclear as to what emotions I was trying to numb but I felt the pain of whatever came up for me in the moment.

I felt like a party was not as much fun when I wasn't able to have a drink. And, sometimes with sober eyes, I saw how alcohol really does impair our judgment. Believe me, when you are the only un-drunk one at the party, the jokes are not that funny, the stories are not that interesting and the singing, if someone starts that, is not usually as good as the singers think. Trust me....you can't sing when you're drunk, but you can have fun trying.

If you are a drinker or drug user, are you able to go to a party and not imbibe? If not, what do you think is holding you back from doing so? What emotion is it that you might be avoiding so you drink or do drugs to numb yourself? Ask yourself, listen for the answer and make the changes necessary to be healthy. Your body will tell you how.

If I went out to dinner with my girlfriend and she was having a glass of wine, I was really tempted to have a drink too but, I knew that if I could just get past that invitation of alcohol, say no thank you to the waiter and not eat the bread, even when I was starving, I would be okay. Giving up alcohol was also a benefit when I finally realized that dinner without it was affordable and could even be inexpensive. It was easy to decide what to choose from the menu because so much of it I no longer ate. More than once the waiter laughed when I ordered the frozen water soup and a watercress salad, no dressing, hold the cress. For a main course, I'd ask for the imported hailstones, sautéed in seawater and served over a bed of thinly sliced ice cubes. I'd often order water lily roots and request the fresh watermelon for dessert but ask them to put it on the side and bring me the pits because them, I could eat.

The discipline that I was displaying in having a strict and cleaner diet along with my intention to learn how to take care of myself was making me feel proud of myself. I decided to look into becoming a macrobiotic and after reading Wendy Esko's *Introducing Macrobiotic Cooking* (Japan Publications, Inc., August 1989,) I signed up for a class to learn more about this healing lifestyle.

Macrobiotics is a philosophy which promotes health and happiness through balance and harmony on a physical and spiritual level. It is said that you can achieve this state of balance by eating cooked brown rice daily, avoiding anything that comes from an animal along with anything refined, packaged or canned. Eating little raw food, no sugar and no wheat was also important. At the end of the first class, we all had an opportunity to taste everything that had been prepared and the flavour was better than any food I had ever tasted. Everything was delicious, wholesome, natural and organic and spectacular to experience; I loved it.

That night I went home and went to bed not yet realizing what a profound effect this class would really have on my life. When I awoke the next morning, before I opened my eyes I knew that I felt different and quite honestly incredible. It only took a minute to understand that the organics that I had eaten the night before were the reason. I was feeling a deep sense of peace in my body unlike anything I had ever felt in my entire life before. I also felt like I had slept for twenty years in that one night. It was as if every night of my life that I had ever lain awake unable to sleep was made up for. A sense that I had been far away, for a long time filled me and I felt restored. The food which I had been eating that was sprayed with pesticides, included chemicals and was not organic, was something that my body did not like but I had never known this truth. This was an obvious sign telling me to eat organics and I heard it loud and clear. Rip Van Winkle would have been jealous because even though he slept for twenty years in a fairy tale, he could never have felt as good as I did that morning when I woke up.

From that moment forward I committed to eating organic food only and also continued to cook according to the macrobiotic diet until I listened to my body and knew that it was no longer necessary.

Do you sleep well at night? If not, it could even be something that you are eating that causes your insomnia.

Are you overweight? Eating a macrobiotic diet can help you lose weight and eat appropriately for your natural body.

Are you interested in helping Mother Earth? Eating organics is a way to help out there as well.

I knew that caffeine was an unhealthy choice and learned that coffee is a legal drug that is addictive. Caffeine carries essential vitamins from our body through our urine and I had started taking supplements to help build my immune system. I knew that I would have been wasting the time and money I invested in them if I continued to drink coffee, so gave it up. When I thought about it, I realized that it was the social aspect of being with the people and not the coffee itself that I wanted, so I decided to substitute it for something else. I drank soup for the warmth, comfort and health benefits it provided when I socialized each morning with my colleagues. Herbal teas became a part of my diet for the soothing nature they provide and even plain hot water is a delicious source of relaxation that I benefit from.

Do you hear yourself saying that you are unable to start your day without coffee? Are you okay with being addicted to a drink? How do you feel about having to depend on a drug to get you going first thing each morning?

Are the foods you're ingesting really benefiting your health in every way? As you answer and look inside yourself, take responsibility and make the changes you need to in what you eat and you will see that your life will reflect that honouring change in many other ways as well.

For the first time in my life I was trying to be less of a doer and making an effort to be at peace with myself when I was being quiet and not working. Why was it not okay for me to do nothing and why did I feel guilty when I did?

When I was growing up, I was the second oldest girl in a large family and I acted like the nanny, always helping my mother because there was so much going on in a household with nine children. When I was in my teens, my close cousin was over for dinner one night and at the end of dinner offered to help me do dishes. My mother responded by telling her that I would do the cleaning up because I was used to it. If it was up to me, I might have enjoyed the help with the dishes but my mother spoke up for me and declined the offer. That was my typical of my mother. It became part of my belief system as a child that there was always a lot of work to be done, so as an adult I had difficulty relaxing. Only looking back at this, years later, did I realize that being busy constantly is really being in a state of distraction in order to avoid feeling and facing some internally stored emotion. Just like alcohol or drugs, this distraction numbed me. This desire to always keep going and be involved really masked something deeper that I did not want to address. What helped at this crucial point in my journey to healing was that I was so energy-deficient that I had no choice but to sleep more, do nothing and just be. I now had the time to look inside myself.

Do you feel guilty when you are not doing something and keeping busy? If so, what emotion do you think you are trying to avoid feeling? Can you see deeper within yourself and your life experiences and understand why you feel this way? Work on this and it will help you heal.

Thank God I can read and love doing so. The books I was choosing for guidance were my saviour. I read everything I could on disease, nutrition and healing and found they especially helped with my spiritual growth and a major shift in my perception. Shakti Gawain's *Creative Visualization* (Bantam Books, 1979,) and Ken Keyes *Handbook to Higher Consciousness* (Love Line Books, 1975,) made a huge impact on my perception of life and the world and helped me understand that we are all here on a spiritual journey. Gawain teaches how to positively change your life and attain everything that you want by using your imagination to visualize your dreams, just like *The Secret*. She encourages us to let go of control, surrender, meditate and visualize and illustrates these concepts with practical exercises.

I utilized the exercises in her book to help achieve my goals and began to write affirmations. An affirmation is a short, strong positive statement which affirms a goal and helps you imagine that it is happening already. In other words, I learned that if I wanted something, by affirming it over and over and experiencing the energy of it happening now, in this moment, it will happen.

For example, if I wanted to move, I would write an affirmation that would help like: "I now am living in my affordable, two bedroom apartment in High Park". Putting it into the present tense, I feel the energy of it as a reality. Sometimes I would write affirmations, put them away in my wallet and carry them with me. After forgetting about them, I would eventually retrieve them months later to find myself delighted and surprised when I saw that I had changed the things I had been affirming to change. I could see that when I put the energy of a desire out into the universe, it is an easy way to practice being positive and receive my intention.

Do you have any goal that you would like to attain? Do you want to become more positive in your outlook on the world? Writing and saying affirmations helps in this way.

I began to think more positively, set goals for myself and ask for the things I wanted. I wanted to learn to unblock myself and stop holding myself back from being successful. At the time, I didn't know what that meant but I did understand that with the extraordinary artistic talent that I was given in this lifetime, I felt I should be more prosperous. I definitely did feel that I was blocking myself but was unable to get to how or why this was happening.

Simple, positive affirmations are powerful to repeat even if I do not have any specific goals I want to attain. For example, "Every day in every way I am getting better and better" and "I now am living a fulfilled, prosperous life". I would repeat these affirmations and picture their reality, feeling the emotions as if I was there already and I inevitably felt better.

I also tried to stop controlling the outcome of everything and began to believe that I was being guided. In the past, I would have prayed to resolve a relationship with a boyfriend so we could be together again. But with this new belief system I was adopting, I would now affirm or pray for the most appropriate outcome for everyone involved, letting go of control. If that meant that we would not be able to settle any issues, then the universe knows better than me, and so does my soul. Everything always works out for the best in the end. This was a shift in me and working on letting go of control is something that made a big impact in my life. I could see that I got more work done each day once I let go of control. I began to see that the most important things that were necessary to get accomplished each day always did and that the things on my list that I didn't get to, I could do tomorrow. There was much peace in this shift for me and it works to be able to go with the flow through each day.

Because we only know what we are taught by our parents, we grow up learning to control and manipulate others around us to get them to do what we want. I had a friend who would often call me and ask me to go shopping with her as she did not enjoy this weekly event. Sometimes, I would accommodate her but other times I did not want to or just did not feel like going out so would have to continue to find new and creative ways to say no, thank you. She would continue to ask me, attempt to talk me into it and just not take no for an answer. And, at times she was successful. I realized much later in life that when someone does not take no for an answer, they are trying to control you. "No" is a perfectly appropriate response and with respect for each other it is and needs to be acceptable to all of us.

Can you see any ways in your life where you are controlling things? Do you ever find yourself not accepting someone else's no? Stop trying to control others and just let go.

One of the most effective things that I have done to heal myself was to commit to really taking care of myself and make the changes that were necessary to accomplish this. I was disciplined and worked hard to see the world in a different, more positive way by reading books, eating more balanced, organic food and meditating to find peace and joy. I began to notice when I was triggered by something and went deeper to the feelings that lay underneath that trigger and my behaviour and now I understand; it is the stored, unfelt emotions that will come to the surface and need to be felt to heal these wounds.

Spending quiet time alone every day with my emotions and speaking out loud to those people I feel hurt by allows the toxic emotions to leave my body so that I can heal as I release them. Change will happen if you want it to and every little step helps as you move forward on your journey through life, because believe me, you too are on a journey.

Ask for and want change because it helps.

3. don't give up

If you are going through hell, keep going.

-Winston Churchill

When my doctor left her practice to go on sabbatical, I found a new specialist in Haematologist Pathologist Dr. Alison Bested and began a doctor/patient friendship that would grow over many years. During our initial appointment, I was unable to get through a sentence remembering my words because of brain fog and short term memory loss. She recognized how sick I was and insisted I stay home from school the next day and not go back at all until I was better. So, I took a leave of absence from teaching for a year and believed that the rest that I would get in that time would help provide me with the healing I needed. After all, I had been working very hard all my life even as a child helping my mother and all through college and university I worked part-time to earn my tuition. I was tired and needed some time off –or that was what I thought.

The Board of Education I worked for had offered disability insurance which I had purchased over the years and this would help me pay my mortgage for the year I was on leave. I could finally relax somewhat, knowing I had the time to meditate, eat healthy organics, see a Naturopath, have colonics to detoxify and concentrate on learning to take care of myself. I began to read the contents on packaging of everything and if any food item had more than four or five ingredients, I wouldn't buy it because it wasn't clean enough to put in my body. I took the time to learn about illness and healing and practice what I learned.

Because I had difficulty taking it easy and continued to run even when I didn't want to, Dr. Dean had recommended that I see a behavioural therapist to help me deal with my attitude towards life. I felt disappointed in my body because it had not been as strong and resilient as I wanted it to be. I was now aware of this being an old habit and I knew I could change it. I was clear about wanting and expecting results from the changes that I had been making and could not understand why I wasn't seeing any. I was angry with my body for letting me down and my doctor noticed this as we talked about how I kept pushing myself to accomplish things even when I wasn't feeling up to it. I did not know how to be gentle with myself and understood that this behaviour had been modelled by my parents. One day my father actually told me that if he did not worry every day about something, that nothing in his life would ever get done. He believed that it was a part of his daily routine to worry because he had worried, probably, for his entire life. I learned that from him.

My behavioural therapist, Josephine Newman helped me to see that I was being very hard on myself. I loved going to see her. She would make me tea, let me talk, listen and feel empathy towards the challenges I faced. I felt like I had someone on my side who understood me and she helped me see that my worry was irrational. She taught me to ask myself what was the worst that could happen. Why do we worry anyway? Sometimes getting more information about an issue and more details to clarify helps.

I believe now that we really worry because we lack trust. We have not yet seen that everything always does work out for the best and we don't trust that the universe will provide us with what we need. That is the truth and I was just beginning to understand that what this illness brought me was an opportunity to practice trusting.

Take a minute and look back at your life; everything has always worked out even though I know you have had challenges like me. So, in the future, stop worrying, let go and trust that all will work out.

If we are worriers, we would benefit from learning to have faith in the positive. My parents did not have this belief system, so I watched them worry about things and took on their habit. It is just a habit and it can be changed. I learned to ask myself in every situation that I worried about, what was the worst that could happen and if I could live with that, which I always could, then I would be just fine. I knew I'd somehow work it out. So, I gradually began to trust and stop worrying.

Are you a worrier? Try to alter your perception and see every challenge as an opportunity to believe that it will all work out. Try to not control things and know that what is in the best interest for everyone will occur because it always does. Worrying does not alter the outcome of anything so hand it all over to your spiritual guides to handle, and stop causing yourself stress.

When I was worried, it was often difficult to sleep well and sometimes I would fall asleep but wake up in the middle of the night because my mind was still busy going over the events of the day. When I took The Relaxation Response course with Eli Bay, he taught a progressive relaxation technique that is a very effective, powerful tool to calm the body and helps ensure a good night's sleep. The concept behind it is that it is impossible to fall asleep if you have any tension in your body. I would listen to his soothing voice on tape as he took me through this technique which involves slowly tensing and then releasing each muscle group in your body. I start from the muscles in my head, forehead, eyelids, cheeks and lips and work down my body until I finish at my toes.

PROGRESSIVE RELAXATION

Do you have difficulty sleeping? Try this technique and release the tightness in your body's muscles by slowly tensing and holding them in extreme tension for a few seconds, squeezing them tight, holding, holding, then release until that muscle feels relaxed.

Start at the top of your head and move onto each group of muscles as you work your way down your body to your shoulders, arms, torso, and legs finishing at your toes. You will feel deeply relaxed and be able to drift off to peaceful sleep after this. It works, its natural, it's a way for you to take care of yourself and it's better than taking medication to sleep. Give it a try.

During that first year after I left my job at the Board of Education, my physical energy level was really the marker for how I measured my health and I was still exhausted and not seeing any consistent improvement. Some days I was fine to get up and exercise early in the morning and then later not be able to accomplish much more than just lying down. I knew I was having a good day energy-wise when I could meditate sitting up, while other days I would only be able to meditate lying down. Sometimes, I felt better and could go grocery shopping and do some work around my house. I felt strongly that I needed to move my body, so I continued to exercise as often as possible. I believed that when I finally healed, having worked out daily would be better for me and I see now that it was one of the best decisions I made as I was trusting my intuition.

You may feel that you are symptom-free but everyone needs to exercise to be healthy. Are you doing some form of work out several times a week?

Are you finding excuses to not exercise? If so, why are you not taking care of yourself in this way? You are the only one that can, so look at yourself and make a commitment to loving you.

As time went on, my monthly test results for Candida were showing that the yeast overgrowth in my body was closer to normal yet my symptoms had not improved. Dr. Bested realized that I also had Chronic Fatigue Syndrome, or CFS. CFS is characterized by extreme physical and mental fatigue, inability to sleep well, joint aches and pains, depression and irritable bowel syndrome among other symptoms. This had not been evident before because many of the symptoms are shared with those of Candida Albicans.

The cause of CFS is multi-factorial but it can be triggered by a car accident, stress, a pregnancy, or trauma like a fall down the stairs. It can come on suddenly and last for three months or go on for years. Many people never recover from CFS and are never able to return to work; they just learn to live with it. I knew that learning to live with it was not an option for me because I had just come out of so many years of constantly feeling lousy and I knew that I would do whatever it took to get better. I needed to work again, to make money, to have a life and to be healthy. This illness was only temporary, I believed, and I would never give up trying to heal it by learning to pace myself, save my energy through balance and getting plenty of rest, staying committed to myself and my journey.

Do you need to commit to yourself in some way? Do you need to take responsibility for your health because you are seeing symptoms telling you something? Go for it and don't give up. The answers are out there for you.

I see now how ridiculous it was to have decided to be better in the time frame of a year, but back then I just thought I was really tired. Maybe I was learning patience when I did not improve quickly. Does anything really happen as quickly as we want it to anyway? Was my lesson here to never stop trying?

I am very curious by nature so the mystery of how and when I became ill also was intriguing me. Did I have a virus that I caught from someone at some point in my life? Had I been born with this immune dysfunction? I was not only going to find the answers but I was going to cure myself.

At that point, I was supposed to be returning to work but I really wasn't feeling much better than I did a year earlier. My energy level fluctuated often and was still just 3 out of 10. This was measured intuitively each month when my doctor would ask me how I felt and to rate my vitality. I would also bring samples and have blood tests done, then we would discuss what I was doing to heal, boost my immune system and feel stronger.

Although I was having some better days, my progress seemed to be random and it was not just my energy that was low, but my other symptoms would also flare up. As I worked hard to improve, I could be feeling great sometimes for a week, weeks or even a month, then fall back and relapse and my condition was again like it had been months before. It became very disheartening through the years when I felt like I was making some improvement, then suddenly be set back and unable to do much when my symptoms worsened yet again. This inconsistency in healing CFS is also characteristic of the disease I understand now. So, I realized my plan of returning to school at the end of a year was just a dream when I was not yet well enough.

My chronic concern was over money and the school board disability insurance that I had been living on all year, along with my savings, was quickly dwindling away. I knew I couldn't work, I had no money coming into my life and I would soon be unable to pay my mortgage. I felt such panic. I was in hell and I did not know what to do.

I understand now that I was in the Dark Night of my Soul and it would not be the last time I would have to go there. This happens when you feel like you are in hell on earth and the darkness seems too much to bear. Having been there many times, I know all about it and know that in order to reach a higher level of consciousness, my soul has to sometimes be in that dark place. I feel complete despair, fear, sadness, panic and it's dark until I crack and somehow get through it. Then the light enters me again and I feel relieved. Once I feel myself lighter and happier, I have arrived on the other side and I am more enlightened as a result. For me, this usually manifests itself in some feeling of confusion and uncertainty about things but I always end up becoming stronger in my spiritual self after the transition back from this soul healing.

Have you ever been in the Dark Night of your Soul? Some of us will only have to experience it once in our lives. Others may never have to go there. I have had to go often to learn my lessons. If this happens to you, try to remember it won't last forever and you too will come through it and be better. Hold on, don't judge the process and don't give up. It's all worth it in the end.

When your immune system is challenged or broken down, like mine was, there could also be other factors in your living and work space contributing to your ill health. Environmental Illness is difficult to diagnose in people but my doctor also understood that I could be suffering the effects of exposure to toxic moulds, chemicals, poor air circulation and low quality water in my life. After becoming aware, I did not enter a grocery store for many years because of the fumes, odours and off-gassing from household cleaners and laundry additives which silently leak into the air. I was vulnerable in a toxic place like that, so I stayed away. Newly upholstered furniture and new mattresses have dust, mould and fumes which also leak out and so I learned to buy floor models because they had been previously unpackaged and had released much of their invisible poison.

Learning more about CFS by going deeper into the causes and effects of it helped me educate myself and gave me hope that I really could heal. I was steadfast in my resolve to get better so continued to search for the answers I needed.

I felt such relief when I found that I could apply for disability benefits through the government social services plan because I knew I couldn't work and felt I was a perfect candidate for it. When I sent in my application I also sent verification of my condition from my doctors in the form of letters and hoped for what I thought would be a positive response. When however, I heard back from them, my application had been rejected. They explained that it appeared I was making progress in my healing and should be back to work soon.

This is an example of how there is a lack of knowledge and understanding about CFS in the medical profession and in the community but I was not about to take no for an answer. Maybe perseverance is a gift that some of us are given in our life and maybe some of us have to work at having it. I always believed that I could be healthy and I was ready to do whatever it took to make it happen. It wasn't always easy but I was never going to give up so I appealed their decision by writing an impassioned letter re-explaining the details of my situation. I also had no means of support and needed money to live so I was determined to get their help. I had gone from a hard-working, self-sufficient, single woman to someone with no income, no energy to work and no means of support. How was I supposed to heal? As I waited to receive their answer I put myself on a strict budget because I was in a pretty poor financial state.

Throughout that winter I decided that the $2500 which I was

going to need to heat my house was an expense I could not afford, so I kept the temperature down at 60 degrees Fahrenheit all the time. This made it pretty cool in the house but warm enough to not freeze, which was maybe great for a squirrel. In the spring someone from the gas company called me in a ploy to entice me to switch from oil for heating, which was expensive at the time, to the much cheaper gas. I remember that day, because it was March and my ass was just beginning to defrost. It had cost me $600 for heat for the entire winter and I got through it by believing I could and taking it on as a challenge. I wasn't going to let a little frost-bite on my bum bother me.

Finally, six agonizing, long months later, I heard back from social services and they decided this time to accept my appeal. I would be receiving $700 a month, which would enable me to pay rent on a one bedroom apartment but the balance of money I needed to live, would have to come from somewhere else. My medical costs, food, phone and even laundry detergent were not in that budget. I had saved and hidden $1500 in an account in order to have first and last month's rent on an apartment but first I had to sell the house. A real estate agent coming through my place one day noticed a foul smell coming from the basement and I discovered it was a broken sewer line between my house and the street caused by a neighbour's tree roots. The $1500 that I had saved for rent was used to repair this so that I could sell the house without a poop-filled basement. When I was left without any money for my apartment, I applied for Unemployment Insurance and this gave me enough for my first and last because while I was waiting to sell the house, I completely ran out of money.

It took eight months for the house to go and in that time I could not pay my mortgage because both my disability insurance and savings were gone. I spoke to my bank several times about this, explaining my situation so that they were aware of why my mortgage was not being paid and when I finally did sell, it was at a loss of $33,000. I knew that I owed the bank that money and would probably have to declare personal bankruptcy to deal with it because I certainly could not pay it then. However, after looking into the bankruptcy issue, I decided to wait until I was approached by them at some point in the future to handle it, so I held off on declaring bankruptcy immediately. I did not have the energy to do anything then anyway, so decided to trust that eventually it would all work out.

I really could not understand why I was not better after working so hard at it but it just made me become more determined to find out why. It seemed to be taking such a long time but I can see now that I was not only going deeper inside myself to find a quiet place to heal but also practicing a deeper commitment to the time and effort it would take me to get there. I continued to read and learn more about Candida and CFS from my doctors and by researching. I stayed away from grocery stores, went for colonics to detoxify, tried to not worry, and kept searching for a solution. As my spirituality was growing so was a closer contact with God. The fear I felt about not being able to return to work in a year's time and running out of money to live really catapulted me into intense emotions that tested my commitment to myself. But what else could I do? It was curiosity and interest in solving the mystery of where and when this illness was created that kept me going, learning and healing, I think now. I decided to stay committed to the truth that I was on a spiritual journey instigated by my health challenges and everything I learned as

I read and did research helped me do this. I was never going to give up my quest to discover how to heal.

4. trust

Trust even if you cannot see. That's how faith must be.

-Unknown

After spending two years on a leave of absence from school, my health continued to improve so slowly that I knew I would not be able to go back to work in the foreseeable future. I decided to resign from the Board and believed I was leaving teaching forever; I swore I'd never go back.

Unconsciously, I felt like it had broken me and the intensity and hard work involved in the profession had contributed to my becoming sick. At the time, I did not know how to take responsibility for creating this illness, and I was blaming but also looking for answers.

Eventually, I would come to know that there is no blame and that I am accountable for myself in every way. I had to learn to trust the process of my journey even though at times I was uncomfortable with where I was. Maybe being able to take care of myself has been the biggest learning curve I've experienced in this lifetime. I was beginning to see that I was on earth living a human experience and to learn to trust that God has a divine plan for me; for everyone. But, I had never trusted that things would work out for me, because I chose to be a victim and only saw that life was difficult, usually painful and always involved a struggle of some kind. Of course, now I know that my parents clearly were 'in victim' and they modelled that notion.

We are all conditioned by how we are brought up but it is never too late to learn another, more positive way to view life.

Looking back I also see that I probably always felt alone. That is not to say lonely, just unsupported and challenged by the weight of a sense of being by myself, feeling abandoned. Later, through Coaching I knew that this too was a state that came about because I did not know how to support myself, and so the universe was reflecting those feelings of abandonment back to me. It's not surprising that when I began to quiet myself and listen, I would intuitively start to hear the whispers of the backup I so craved from the universe through my angels and guides.

I was working on connecting to my journey by turning my awareness inward and once I decided to believe, I immediately felt the presence of my angels guiding me. I had obviously ignored them before, but now I knew to try to trust that I was being watched over.

I had been reading about angels in Doreen Virtue's books, *Healing with the Angels*, (Hay House Publishing, 1999), out of interest and curiosity. She has communicated with angels for many years and writes books, teaches courses and lectures and describes her experiences with them as normal conversations filled with an abundance of important information for everyone. She talks about how our belief systems dictate what we attract into our lives and that when we see the universe as only love, then, it will be evident to us that God wants us to be happy, abundant, and prosperous and to live with no pain or limitations. We will attract what we believe in.

Her work also helped me become sensitive to my intuition and I began learning how to listen to that small, quiet voice inside that guides me and that is never wrong. I began to see that intuition, creativity and spirituality are all intermingled, and so understood that my creativity and artistic talent had a spiritual basis. I had never put those two together before but I now knew that my creative problem solving skills came from a divine source. I had always been able to brainstorm and come up with ideas for anything I was thinking about doing and I later appreciated that this was my ability to channel. Channelling is where we connect to our higher selves or a higher power and the high-level vibration is available for us to download and use. I believe we all channel but some of us are not aware of doing it or get that it comes from a divine source.

Somehow, I think that Doreen Virtue's belief and relationship with angels inspired me also to believe; after all, she was a very well-known Ph. D. and I'm not alone in trusting that she is truthful about her experiences. Being brought up Catholic has also given me spiritual roots and I was learning to see the world in a new way because of these new views. I decided to speak out loud to my angels one day when I needed help, after my Naturopath told me that our voice box is situated so close to our hearts that when we speak, the vibration of the words immediately connects us to divinity. That means that when I talk with positive intention, God and the angels hear me right then. I loved knowing this because I believed it instantly and began to ask for help, trusting that there would be an answer, signs, whispers and happenings that I would recognize coming from my guides in the spirit world. What did I have to lose?

- Am I really being watched over by my angels?
- Do they see me when I'm naked?
- Can they hear me and will they help me if I ask them for it?

I decided to try and see what would happen; to trust that something would – and it did. I began to ask for help with everything from my angels either by my thoughts, telepathically or by talking to them and I noticed really quickly that I would get a response immediately when I spoke out loud. Some kind of sign or answer is always there for me and it comes in through my thoughts, what I see or what I hear. I became immediately hooked on communicating with my angels this way and feel no shame or embarrassment when I talk to them in front of other people asking them questions and receiving answers. This is not only how I get my answers but I can tell you I have never felt alone since then, knowing that they are with me, supporting me and guiding me. And, it's so much fun.

We are all born with at least two guardian angels that stay with us throughout our lifetime to help and guide us. We also have spirit guides that come to us from the spiritual world and are entities – not physical – who provide us with support, guidance and assistance from another realm. Why had I been ignoring mine all my life when I should have been tapping into that resource right beside me? I had often noticed many instances where I was protected and believed it was my guardian angel, but never made an effort to cultivate a relationship with her or them. Why not? I had been missing out.

Once on my way to school early in the morning, I was driving too fast and on a highway curve moving onto an onramp when my car skidded. I felt it going out of control with what I immediately foresaw was going to be a very serious accident. The car, however, suddenly straightened out and I knew that it was a miracle. In my mind's eye I clearly saw a large female hand over the roof of my vehicle, grab it from above and straighten it out. At the time, I had no idea that I was clairvoyant and that I was actually seeing a vision of what really saved me that morning.

All my life I had been seeing visions like this one, but I just thought that it was because I was a visually oriented person. I assumed that others saw them too. As I began to quiet myself and listen, I had these pictures more frequently and I knew that day, that it was my guardian angel who had been there for me.

I also felt my deceased mother's spirit was there to help. I have always remembered the experience like it was yesterday. I was probably moving too quickly through my life, numbed by the busyness and too distracted to really notice this angelic guidance, but my angels intervened many other times to protect and help me. Then, I would just go back to ignoring them and didn't focus on their presence. Now, I had the time, inclination and interest because I was curious and listening.

I had been aware of feeling my mother's presence for many years since her death at 42. After people close to us die, like my mother, they become an angel to us and are with us to help protect and guide us. I would think of her and talk to her, and not only felt her presence but knew she was watching over me. I still often feel her.

Seventeen years after she died, I had purchased a black sweater that I thought would look great accessorized with a strand of pearls. I suddenly received an image of the time when I was organizing her belongings to give away after her death. I remembered finding a strand of pearls among her things which at the time, I threw into a small bowl with some other costume jewellery. I had completely forgotten about it and wondered why I suddenly remembered and saw its image seventeen years later. I assumed the pearls were costume, because I don't recall ever seeing my mom wear pearls, nor could she ever have afforded real ones. But, I dug them out of the bowl they had been sitting in for so many years, the one I had forgotten about, and took a look at them. I tested them to see if they were real, by dragging them across my front teeth because they say that if you can feel the grittiness from the sand in the pearl, it's authentic. I was shocked to discover that they were real pearls so took them to a reputable jeweller to have them restrung. They confirmed that they were real and probably worth about $600. They had been sitting in a bowl in my closet for so many years and now became one of the most beautiful, heaven-sent pieces of jewellery that I own. I really felt like this was a gift from heaven sent by my mother when she reminded me through a memory thought that those pearls were there waiting. Again, a sense of knowingness gave me confidence that this incident too showed me that she was with me, watching over me. I trusted her presence.

Do you ever feel the presence of your guardian angel? Do you ever feel the presence of one of your deceased relatives? Believe it when you suddenly think of your grandmother who has passed, for example, and believe that she is there with you sending you that reminder of her. Talk to her and ask her for help from the other side. Trust she will answer and then listen with your heart to hear or feel her responses.

Do you find yourself ever suddenly noticing the smell of flowers or the smell of your grandfather's pipe? Angels are with you when you notice these scents, so speak to them and feel their presence. They too will send you messages if you ask them. You can practice building a relationship with them by doing this and it's fun to play with your invisible friends.

My angels really came in handy when I needed them to help me find things I was constantly misplacing because I was so foggy-headed from being toxic. I was overwhelmed and keeping my space at home clean and clear seemed to be a challenge because I so often couldn't find important things I needed; notes I had written, receipts, a letter, a pair of earrings. I knew they weren't lost; I just was unable to find them when I needed to do so. I did not know then that angels could have a special job, but I knew that I needed them to help me locate whatever I had lost, so I asked them for their help out loud. Only later did I understand that Locator Angels are with us to help us find what we need. My confidence in them grew when I started getting their answers and guidance to help find things and I learned to trust that they were working with me.

Once I needed to buy something in the grocery store and I had to go and get in and out quickly because I was feeling my energy fade and it wasn't a healthy place for me to be for any length of time. This was a common occurrence at the time. I felt the need to get home before I collapsed or just passed out. Time was of the essence, so I found my way to the aisle after asking for help and stood where I knew the food item I was looking for was shelved. I asked my angels for help finding it so that I could grab it and go. But as I stood there, I was unable to see it anywhere. I continued to scan the shelves and ask my angels for help but I was so tired and when I couldn't find it, I decided to leave. Just then something extraordinary happened. Suddenly, I felt two strong but gentle hands on my shoulders turn me around in a 360 degree move and when I spun around, there it was, right in front of me. It had been in that aisle right behind me as I stood searching. I knew it was my angels answering my requests for help but the reality of it took my breath away and I started laughing. They were with me and showed me and I really trusted that they would be there for me again, and they have been. This is the kind of response I got after deciding to talk out loud with them in a firm belief that they were with me.

Do you ever have unexplained happenings like the one I describe here? If and when you do, because I believe you do, then know that it is your angels helping you. If you begin to talk to them and thank them, they will make their support clearer to you in the future.

Don't be afraid to ask your angels for help or talk to them. They are with you for that and it is their job; all they want in return is a thank you.

Today when I lose or misplace something, I know that it is a reminder from my angels that I was not being present when I put it away. Now, I know that it is a part of everyone's journey to learn to stay in the moment throughout the day but that it is a great challenge for most of us.

Have you ever gone to the refrigerator to get something and forgotten what it was when you get there? Have you ever moved from your living room to the bedroom to grab something you needed only to realize once there, that you can't remember what it was you came for?

Have you ever picked up your running shoes to put away in your gym bag and then put them in the refrigerator instead? Then, later wonder why you can't find them? When we do these things, we are not being present.

An effective affirmation that helps when I feel myself not present and am reminded with a frozen pair of running shoes, for example, is to say, 'I am here, I am here, I am here.' This brings me back to the present and helps me be right where I am, in the moment, and aware that my consciousness is fully with me.

Being present is a part of learning to trust. Sometimes reminding myself by talking out loud helps bring me back to the moment. I say 'I am putting my glasses down on my dresser.' This helps so that the next time I am looking for my glasses, I don't wander around my apartment searching only to finally find them inside a frozen shoe in my gym bag in the freezer. Probably what takes us away from being fully in the moment are the thoughts of the future or past that we are concerned or worried about. Our anxious thoughts keep us from being here, right now; being present in the moment.

Once we learn to trust that everything is perfect and that there is a divine plan for us, and to let go of the outcome, then we will learn to be present. If we stay present and let the day unfold without trying to control it, we have learned an important lesson.

Remember to affirm often, 'I am here'.

As I continued to experiment communicating with them, I discovered that I could speak to my angels with just a thought. I was sure I was receiving clearer results from asking out loud, but inside my head or telepathically works too. I began writing in a journal to ask for angel help and also asked for their help in my meditations. I often ask them to send me the truth of a life situation I am challenged by through a dream and request their help on how to resolve it. Once I decided to believe in my angels, it was like they had been there anxiously awaiting my awareness; I felt them with me immediately.

I used my angels as my built-in alarm clock for years as I tested them and worked on building our connection. I knew I needed to trust that they would wake me up so I used my real alarm clock at first as a backup. The first night I tried this, I asked them out loud to 'please wake me up before my alarm clock goes off.' I learned a lesson that night the hard way when I understood that I needed to be very specific when asking for help because they woke me up every two hours throughout the night. That is also when I realized that my angels have a sense of humour because although I had a sleepless night, I thought it was funny and felt them laughing along with me. After all, they did what I had asked them to. So, I learned quickly to be clear and the next night I asked specifically that they 'please wake me at 6:30 a.m. before my 6:40 a.m. alarm.' This worked and each morning that they awakened me before my alarm was a gift because I saw that they were present and I was trusting.

At other times, my angels have been creative in finding ways to wake me. Noises which come from a piece of furniture in my bedroom will wake me. These sounds seem like the wood in the furniture or the drawers in my dresser are suddenly shifting and it is quite loud. This has been happening for many years and as I upgrade and change one piece of furniture which makes the noise, the sound moves on to another. I believe that this is a way for them to communicate with me and because it usually happens in the morning I use it as an opportunity to say hi to them because I feel like they are saying good morning to me.

One morning I woke up because I heard the distinct sound of a newspaper being dropped as if being delivered to my open bedroom door yet, there was no sound of the delivery person's footsteps walking away. It was an angel. I live alone, have no pets and there was no one else in my apartment. That invisible newspaper delivery person I knew was an angel there to help me wake up. About a week after that, a silent alarm went off in my head while I was sleeping and it woke me before my real alarm clock rang. It rang in my head loudly but without making any real audible noise outside in my room. My angels were showing me all the different ways in which they could wake me up to teach me that they were there for me and to be open to lots of interesting alarms. I was having fun learning to trust them. Sometimes they would work my internal alarm into a dream I was having. Once I dreamt that I was in a gym watching a basketball game with hundreds of people. The sound of someone scoring a basket and everyone rising to cheer rang in my head and woke me up exactly when I should have been getting up.

Experiment with your angels by asking them to wake you up in the morning but be specific and see what they do to get your attention. You can begin to build a relationship with your guardian angels this way and it is fun getting to know them. They are there to help you; it's their job.

The time when my angels really showed their presence was when I was doing a deep cell detoxification program several years later. Even though I had been eating organic, clean food and taking care of myself for quite a while, I was still toxic and continually looking for new ways to clear out my body of old poisons. Dr. James Martin, a Naturopath from Sarasota, Florida, developed a system called Nutriscan, which scans the energy changes in our organs and indicates how much stress a particular organ is in due to toxicity. When I became involved in doing this detox, I sent a frozen urine sample once a month to Florida and they evaluated the results. I took about 300 supplements a week but began to see some results myself within a few weeks as communication with my angels became enhanced and my ability to sense, hear and know what they were saying was suddenly magnified. It was like the volume had been turned up. The information I was receiving was clearer, sharper and faster in getting to me and my angels would also answer me back in thoughts, in what I'd hear and in visions. I was certainly feeling less alone in my life and was aware of their ongoing support and guidance and I trusted in a divine plan for me that they were helping me to see.

I certainly had to trust that everything would be fine after I moved from my house and into my apartment, because I had to find some way to survive. I needed cash for living expenses, food, phone, doctors' bills, colonics, treatments, practitioners, therapists, supplements and medical tests. My monthly disability only paid my rent. While teaching, I had been freelancing small art and design jobs for many years, sometimes working with a friend, Diana Abbott who owned an event planning company, Activities Inc. Because I was more available now, she began to hire me more often for part-time, freelance design work for her firm. It was random and perfect as I was able to earn some money for my ongoing medical costs, yet rest a lot in between jobs.

At the time, I knew that the income I made freelancing for her was a godsend and saved my life, but, now I know that it would have been less stress for me if I had just trusted; trusted in God's divine plan, because looking back what I needed just flowed into my life when I needed it. I wasn't ready yet to know this truth. I was grateful, but worried about whether the work would continue or not. I was still worrying. This is the nature of freelancing though, as you never know where or when the next job will come to you. At one point, I wanted to hand it all over to my angels so I decided to trust in the universe and let go. I let go of my trepidation about jobs and money to God and the angels and asked them to bring in the work I needed so I could live because I did not want to worry about it anymore.

Do you have trouble sleeping at night because you worry about money or your job? Do you sometimes hear yourself running over and over some problem in your head that keeps you from being present and relaxed enough to sleep?

A good exercise to practice letting go is my Heart Technique.

HEART TECHNIQUE

- Sit or lie down in a comfortable position and close your eyes.
- Take several long, slow, deep, natural breaths in and out as you count down from three to one, feeling your relaxation growing deeper and deeper.
- Think of a problem you have or a goal that you would like to manifest and picture it as if it has already happened. Imagine the issue resolved in your mind, and see it as clearly as you possibly can. Picture it and focus on it, feeling and sensing what it will be like when it has been achieved.
- Now, surround that goal with the shape of a heart as you connect it to your loving self through your heart by doing this. Let it go and watch it float off into the universe handing it over to god and the angels to take care of.
- Symbolically you released it and the universe is helping it collect positive energy to manifest itself. Let it go emotionally as well and you will see positive results because that is the way to set it free and set yourself free too.

The additional money I was making working freelance was essential for my ongoing medical needs and it gave my spirit something to be excited doing as I learned about the corporate world and the event planning industry. Without this freelance income, there would have been no help and no healing. The government allows anyone receiving disability to gross an additional $10,000 annually to help supplement their monthly disability payments, so people can work a little if they feel up to it. I knew that I was sometimes receiving more than this amount annually but, I claimed it on my income tax, trusting that I would be able to deal with it later, once I was healthy. I did always want to be honest with what I was bringing in. I see now that I had no other recourse than to trust that everything would work out eventually because I needed to heal and I needed money to do it.

When I look back now at all those years I was so sick, I see that things fell into place and that if I had just trusted, I would have known that God had a divine plan for me and that I was in good hands. I wasn't ready to let go of my fear yet and was not yet ready to learn that lesson and being in those challenging situations was what gave me the opportunity to practice trust. I know now that that is one of the most important lessons of my life is to totally trust that I am taken care of by the universe and am always supported.

But maybe it goes deeper than that too. Maybe I needed to recognize my own need for trust at a deeper level within myself. Did I trust myself? Did I believe in myself?

Do you need to trust someone? If we don't trust ourselves, then it is impossible to trust anyone else. In order to believe in anyone else, we must first believe in ourselves. Do you?

Are you always there for you? Can you trust yourself to always show up for you?

I needed to stay in the moment and trust that the money I had coming in was enough and the money I needed in the future would somehow show up; that was hard for me. I constantly was looking to tomorrow and next month concerned for where I was going and what I would live on when I got there. Trusting that I have enough, where I am in the moment and handing the rest over to God and the angels to deal with is the practice of learning to trust. It is a part of everyone's journey; just trust.

5. i am guided

Hear with your heart, see with your soul, be guided by a hand you cannot hold.

-Unknown

When I look back now, I see that I wandered through life as if I was in a board game and did not know the rules. It becomes much easier to navigate our way on our path through life if we can read the signs that are provided to us along the way to help guide us. This is how we find our way on the divine plan that is ours to follow. Since I learned to recognize the signs I have been able to work through my life with much less struggle and eventually, I learned that everything I attract into my life in the way of experiences, relationships, or issues, all have a message for me. I started to pay attention to everything.

Everything is a sign. I noticed that once I believed this, I began to recognize them. For example, if I wake up in the middle of the night and I am thinking or concerned about something in my life, I often notice a siren in the distance on some far away street in the city. I know that this is a sign that means help is on the way and it is also a message reminding me to hand over my worry to God and the angels, because they are there to help in that moment. Lying awake at night worrying about anything is never going to change the outcome.

Guidance and direction often come in the form of dreams as well. Dreams are from the subconscious so should not be interpreted literally. If you have a dream about a baby or being pregnant, for example, it means the birth of something new in your life, the start of a new idea, or a new job. It could be a sign to show you to pay attention to this new beginning in your life and is a good sign. I know that dreams are sent from heaven to help me on my journey.

One evening when I was at home folding my laundry, I received a phone call from someone who introduced himself as a psychic astrologer and said that he was offering a special on readings he'd do over the phone for $35. At first, I wanted to decline his offer and go back to my work, but something in his voice made me pause and listen. He sounded so sincere, trustworthy and calming, like an angel, so I agreed. I believe now that it was my intuition I was listening to when I made that decision to speak to him. I just had a feeling; something I couldn't describe that told me to take him seriously, so I did. Once he took my information, he promised to call me back in half an hour to read me my results. He also said that after the phone reading, when I sent him my payment of $35, he would send me a written copy of the reading with more details. I felt like he trusted me and so I trusted him. I loved that idea and knew that this opportunity just dropped into my lap and it would be interesting to see what he had to tell me because it came so unsolicited.

Forty minutes later, he called explaining that he had arrived at some interesting information and asked if he could have another ten minutes to process it. Of course, I agreed and while I was waiting, I thought of how I had been asking for a sign that would steer me in a new direction in my life. I was ready for something other than the freelance work I had been doing. My friend in event planning did not need my design help as much anymore and I did not know how to go about getting new work; maybe this would point me down another path. I had been working part-time for six years and my health was improving but still very slowly. I continued to struggle financially as I worked hard to make the additional income I needed to follow through on my health and healing. I only worked when I could. I had wanted change but did not know how to go about making it happen.

Ten minutes later, my psychic astrologer called me back and began to read me the story of my life. He talked about me having an exceptionally sensitive side, that my energy could be spiritual and psychic and that I was prone to powerful insights. When he said this, I trusted that he was accurate because he also told me that my own needs had been put away early in my childhood to take on great responsibilities and that I missed out on being a kid to do so. The truth of this made me believe in him and I saw his gift.

He said that I should find something more settled than the freelance work I was presently doing, and that something with more regular hours and less stress and uncertainty would be better for me. He saw me doing something less creative for a while but instructional and commented that I had been tested. That made me feel like I was being watched over by a higher source and that he was here channelling this information from heaven to help show me the way. This guy was good. He warned against the high level of stored emotion in me and said he recognized that I was very hard on myself and could beat myself up. He said I should do body work like yoga with a female teacher to help release tension and to learn to let go. He continued to say that I could learn to face my fear and that I had the courage to do so, and he saw me working with a supportive woman for a couple of years using a simple technique in a brave way to accomplish this. He saw some pain in the transition, and a short term loss of finances until the pressure came off, but said that I had a creative energy for writing and that people with my master number actualize their dreams often later in life. He also saw me having a creative contact with a larger audience and that the media would be involved; I would be an inspirational speaker because I had amazing power. This information was overwhelming to hear but I knew he was giving me direction. However, I also felt a bit broken at hearing the words he spoke that I knew to be true. I really felt he was an angel and I was being led on a new path answering what seemed to be a call from my soul.

What I heard him saying was three things; find a job teaching, do yoga and get a Coach to help you face your fear. I did not think I had any fear and knew I had the courage to face it, whatever it was. But, how was I going to make all of this happen?

The first step I took was to find yoga classes that were affordable and near my apartment. Through the yellow pages I found a studio that seemed to be close enough so that I could take the subway one stop to get there. I signed up for a series of yoga sessions but the surprise came when I got the address from the yoga teacher and it was a lot closer than I had expected. She lived and taught in a set of buildings beside my own apartment building, on my street, so in fact it took me one minute to run over when I wanted to do a scheduled class. This result was even better than what I could have asked for. I knew when things fell into place so easily regarding yoga that this was a sign that I was being guided and I was aware of the effortless energy it took to achieve this goal.

This was a sign to show me that when things are meant to be, then I do not have to struggle in my life. This was a new concept because I had always had to work so hard to make things happen, or so I thought. This was my belief system. The psychic astrologer had recognized this and told me to stand back and take stock, that I was working against myself and that I would have to change gears to go in a new direction in my life, from commercial to spiritual work.

The way these yoga classes had all fallen into place so easily made me realize that there should never be any struggles in our lives. How had I been creating conflict in my life and why? I was still working on myself on a conscious level and using my brain when this issue later presented itself and I realized that my subconscious was involved. What really made me block myself from feeling that things could be easy in life?

Is this what we call self-sabotage? Do you ever find yourself trying really hard to accomplish something or get in touch with someone to no avail? Maybe that is the universe telling you that you should not go there. Maybe you don't need what you think you need but you don't realize it. This could be your soul telling you that you are not getting anywhere because this choice is not appropriate for you. Watch for the signs and learn to listen to your soul.

Over the next few weeks I knew that I was seeing another sign unfold when I heard about a college in Toronto called the International Academy of Design, not once, but twice. When I was talking to a friend and she mentioned the college, I did not think much of it. However, a week later I met another friend I had grown up with in an art supply store, and the significance of this college became apparent after she told me she had been teaching fashion courses there for a while. She suggested I give the Dean a call to find out more about teaching design classes at the Academy.

I understood immediately that hearing of this college twice in a short period of time was important and I recognized the sign and direction in it. After being in touch with my friend the next day to get the Dean's contact information, I sat quietly at my desk for a few minutes just thinking about the opportunity that was before me. Could this phone call to the Dean change my life? What if she actually hired me to teach there? I was sure that I would never go back to teaching but this was at the college level, something that I had always desired. Could this really be happening so effortlessly? After all, I did need a new job.

I know that whenever an opportunity presents itself and I am unsure of whether to take it or not, I have to at least check it out, because it has shown up in my life for a reason. As I sat there pondering the situation, I suddenly felt kind, gentle hands on my shoulders pushing me forward toward the phone and my angel's voice whispered in my ear 'call her.' I knew I would make that call to the Dean because these words were divine. Within 24 hours I had connected with the Academy, interviewed with the Director of the Computer Graphics Department and was offered and accepted a position teaching a hands-on design course called Design Fundamentals. This again, like the yoga lessons fell into place so quickly and easily that I also learned another lesson. When things are meant to be, they just unfold. This was so smooth and without any pain and I felt determined to be able to stop blocking myself and working so hard against myself in the future. I was seeing that life could be easy.

I began to teach at the International Academy of Design, where I stayed for ten years as a part time instructor and I loved every second of being in the classroom with that mature, talented, creative, dedicated student. I had said that I would never go back to being a teacher but this experience had joy in it every day for me. There seemed to be far less struggle in the classroom as well and each student appreciated and benefitted from my experience both in business, as a working artist and as a teacher. Eventually, I was able to get classes for other design departments also, teaching Visual Communication, Drawing and Portfolio Design and Advertising a few days a week. I was still on disability but continued to need that income I was making to pay for my ongoing medical costs, so I pushed myself to work when I could and rest when I wasn't. My slow healing continued with my determined attitude and the jobs helped a lot. I was grateful.

Several weeks after my good fortune of starting yoga classes and beginning a new teaching position, I was out to dinner one evening and was introduced to a beautiful ex-model, Colleen

Hoffman. We had a brief but interesting conversation as my friend caught up with her and we hugged when she said goodbye and went back to dinner with her new boyfriend. Again, I did not think anything of this meeting but a few weeks later, I remembered that I had one more goal left to achieve out of the three that my psychic astrologer reader suggested – to find someone that would help me face my fear. What was I afraid of anyway? I didn't feel any fear and how was I going to find someone to help me with this?

That night I went to bed and had a good night's sleep but when I woke in the morning, the feeling of that hug I remembered receiving from Colleen the night I met her weeks before was clear and present. I remembered so much love coming through from the heart of a stranger whom I had just met. I thought back to that evening and it came to me very clearly that I was to ask Colleen to coach me and help me face my issues. But, was she really a stranger? I felt so much love from her hug and she felt so familiar to me. It was absolutely obvious and a message sent to me early in the morning when I am open, clear and receptive to hear the truth of things. I decided that I would set up this coaching opportunity with her and I also knew that this was another sign showing me a new direction.

It may have taken me a month or so to call Colleen and it was probably the fear of the cost of sessions that held me back. Again, every penny I was making had to go to my medical costs but I felt that this too would be healing at a deeper level of my soul and maybe I would get to the reasons why I had been holding myself back and struggling, still not healthy in my body. After our first meeting, Colleen wanted to set up more appointments and felt me holding back, afraid of the cost and commitment. I see now that the fear of the cost was not the only reason but deeper inside me there was probably a fear of success and a fear of healing because maybe I didn't really feel I deserved to be healthy. In her gentle heart, she spoke up and told me I had a spiritual commitment to do the work and we had a soul contract. She was not going to let me back out because of fear of not having enough money; that was a fear I had to heal. At that moment I heard my mother speak to me as an angel and she said 'the money will be there.' This gave me the confidence that my mother was helping me and that this coaching was a very important step in my life.

Looking back, I cannot tell you how I ever paid for the coaching sessions and my medical bills, but what I will tell you is, the money for it was always there, just like my mother had promised. And, it was the best thing I ever spent money on in my life because I was truly working with an earth angel who knew exactly how to help me face my fear and heal at a deep level. I was learning to listen to my guides, angels and my intuition and I was getting answers and beginning to recognize what I was afraid of.

Along with recognizing the signs that guided me through the psychic astrologer's phone call, my angels have also shown themselves to me in other ways. One night, I was driving home after a meeting and I had a car accident that was my fault. I had always had a good driving record and had been with the same insurance company for 17 years. No one was hurt and both of us involved were able to drive our vehicles away. Because I am always looking for what my learning is and for the signs around me and what they mean, I tried to figure out what lesson was in this accident. I thought back to the moment before it happened and realized that I had taken my eyes off the road for a second.

Across the street, to my left a man was walking and he appeared to trip and was about to fall. I thought he may be in distress so when he caught my eye, I looked over to see if I could help him and just then, I had the accident. A moment later, that man was not even anywhere around. In *The Secret Language of Signs* by Denise Linn, (Random House, N.Y., 1996) she talks about how accidents occur when we may not be paying attention to the details in our life that guide us. Maybe I felt like I needed to take care of that man on the street, took my eyes off the road and stopped taking care of myself momentarily when I did that.

Was that my lesson? Had I stopped putting myself first and in that moment and had an accident because of it? Was I looking out for everyone else and not myself?

It is a common theme in the spiritual world that accidents are not really accidents at all, so I began to look at myself and try to see if I had really made a subconscious decision to have an accident for some reason. I was not able to see then that I had and I could not figure out at the time why it happened. I also did not see what my lesson was but, because of the additional cost of auto insurance with a new company, I understood that I would have to save money so decided to move to a smaller, more affordable apartment and pare down my life to fit into it.

Did the accident occur because I had decided that I wanted to move but unconsciously did not know how to make it happen? My rent had just gone up and it was costing me more than I thought it should have. Also, I was doing less freelance work and did not need the extra space that apartment had been providing for me. I was teaching at the Academy and see now the connection and the possibility of me creating an accident to in turn set off this chain of events that followed. These are unconscious decisions I could have made.

Can you see how you have created any accidents in your life? Remember, there is no such thing as an accident so you have a hand in it. What is the accident telling you about what you have to learn?

Do you have accidents often? Do you feel accident prone? Make sure to check in with yourself and note whether you are 'in victim' or not. When we choose to be victims, our energy is weakened by the vulnerability that we feel. We forfeit our power or control and that leaves us feeling unsafe. Just relax, meditate and shift your energy taking back your power. It is your choice and you can change it.

Only later did I see that the car accident had caused so many changes that redirected me, guiding me, sending me out to find a new insurance company and a new, smaller, less expensive apartment where I could save some money to pay my increased insurance. Once I decided to move, I went out viewing new places in the area and within 24 hours had secured a one bedroom apartment in a building close to where I had been living since I'd sold my house. I looked at a few apartments but when I walked into one on the ground floor, with a garden that had two walls that were windows, I knew it would be my new home. The space was light-filled and my angels all called out to me in unison 'the light, the light.' Because I am connected to the light and am a Light Worker, light is one of the most important features in every space I spend time in.

Light Workers are on earth on a sacred mission to help others in the world heal from their fear. They agree to this soul contract or life plan before being born and bring the light believing that a spiritual outlook can heal every situation. My angels had guided me again by bringing me to this place where I could start a new phase of my life with lots of light so I could help myself heal my fears.

I was excited about cleaning out all of my closets to move and loved getting rid of the excess that I had accumulated, leaving the energy around me stagnant because I had too much stuff. It is a soul exercise to clean closets, drawers and areas of your life in order to bring in new energy, abundance and prosperity. And only later did I realize that deciding to choose an apartment on the ground floor helped me feel grounded in my body which also had a healing effect. For many years I had enjoyed living up high on the 15th floor because of the view, the quiet and being closer to the clouds. But, I only understood once I decided to live on the ground, connected to Mother Earth that this was where I was supposed to be to be healthy.

Do you ever feel anxious during the day and caught up in the confusion that's going on around you? Are you feeling too hyper to focus at times during your day? Are you aware that you are not completely in your body when you feel stressed or are unable to sleep at night? You are probably not grounded in your body and need to be to feel better.

Here is an exercise that is a wonderful tool to help you feel more grounded:

GROUNDING YOURSELF

- Sit down somewhere comfortable with your feet planted firmly on the ground, close your eyes, have your hands open on your lap and breathe long, slow, deep breaths.

- As you continue to breathe, picture roots growing down deep into the earth from the bottom of your feet like they would from a large, strong oak tree. Imagine them growing thicker and longer and growing deeper into the ground with each breath that you take as you breathe out. Notice your body feeling stronger as it attaches to this strength from deep in Mother Earth.

- Now, continue breathing and with each breath in, begin to see and feel energy coming up through the roots deep in the ground into your body and as you breathe out see that energy leaving from the top of your head and moving into the universe. Imagine that you are breathing in peace, strength and positive energy from Mother Earth up from your feet through your body and out the top of your head.

- Continue breathing this way for five minutes, just one minute or even 30 seconds will help you to feel more grounded, relaxed and less stressed.

- Do this as often throughout the day as you can and you will feel enhanced awareness, relaxation and be calm and stress free. This is a tool that will help you find peace, deal with depression and help you sleep better at night.

Nancy Newman

The things we call coincidence, the dreams we have, our intuition and experiences that happen in our lives are messages and nudges from our soul to redirect us on our pathway through life. We are being guided by them and need to learn how to understand them. When we sleep, we are able to connect to the divine so we are really receiving spiritual information this way through our dreams.

The appointments we make that are cancelled, the trips we book that fall through, the things we lose that we believe we needed, are all signs showing us we didn't need them at all because if we did, we would still have them. When we think we have a really great idea for something and work hard at trying to make it happen but it doesn't, that is our soul telling us that it wasn't such a good idea after all or maybe the time is not now for it to take flight. We think we know but our soul knows better so why not learn to listen to it? We are always being guided by the universe on our journey and there is a divine plan for each of us. We think we know where we are going but we don't really know until we get there. We have to learn to listen and read the signs that show up for us always guiding us on our way every single day.

6. self-worth

Sometimes the hardest part of the journey is believing you're worthy of the trip.

- Glenn Beck

Remember how I didn't think I was afraid of anything? Well, in reality I was afraid of a lot. I realized this when I started to look at myself through Life Coaching with Colleen Hoffman-Smith, author, facilitator and emotional intuitive. It was my lack of self-worth that created my fear. I was afraid to be really truthful with the people I felt disregarded or disrespected by. I would be hurt, then angry and then blame them for being a bully or insensitive – but never speak to them about it. I'd just complain to others.

Have you ever done that? I did not know what being authentic was and I seemed to be attracting people into my life who I felt attacked me and who projected their anger onto me. I did not know how to get the anger I felt out of my body and then speak my truth to them from my heart.

That would have taken someone who loved and believed in

themselves. I was blaming people and did not know how to forgive them or even that I should.

Anger, hurt, guilt and sadness never leave our bodies unless we release those emotions and what most of us do is just push them away, not knowing how to deal with it all. We may even forget about it but that pain is still inside us stored away in our muscles or organs and it will bubble up to the surface at some point when we are triggered or manifest in an illness.

I know now that in order to restore my sense of self-worth I had to heal my own emotional body, heal in all my relationships and be authentic and loving with myself as well as others. I knew that my fears come from my lack of self-worth. It was time for me to learn how to live from my heart and speak my truth. We can all do this by taking care of our own emotions by owning them.

Why did I complain about people's behaviour and but never address it with them? I was afraid of their anger.

Why did I blame others for my issues and think it was their fault? I didn't know how to take responsibility; I was a victim.

Why was everyone else around me wrong, making me the victim? I gave away my power and did not even know it.

None of these situations ever left me feeling anything but uncomfortable.

What is self-worth and where can we get it? Self-worth is the level of inner love and peace we feel for ourselves. We are all born with it and have it when we are babies, but at some point as children we begin to look outside ourselves for this love instead of remembering it is inside us. Maybe this starts when we get to an age where our parents reprimand us for our behaviour and we feel like bad little girls or boys looking to regain their approval.

Maybe they even project their anger onto us because they are tired or worried or have problems. It is never appropriate for anyone to project their stuff on anyone else. Parents do the best they can for us but when we're children and they scold us in anger, we begin to try to be good and fix things to win back their love. This begins our journey away from our own sense of self-worth as we stop loving ourselves and look to others for approval.

Because our parents' self-worth is also lacking, they try to compensate by giving their children the love – trying to constantly fill us up. This is exhausting because it is impossible to do; you can never give anyone enough love to make them feel happy. Parents also look outside themselves for love by thinking that when their child feels better, they too will feel better.

When we are doing things for people to make ourselves feel better, it is our self-worth that is lacking. Being needy for our children is not the same as loving them. If we don't love ourselves, then how can we inspire our children, students or friends to love themselves? Be the love rather than give the love.

How much do you love yourself? Here are a few questions that can reveal your level of self-worth:

- Are you feeling loving and peaceful inside?
- Are you able to forgive others you feel have hurt you?

- Do you blame other people when you feel uncomfortable emotions?
- Do you take responsibility for everything that comes into your life?
- Are you authentic, speaking your truth, having the courage to stand up to bullies?
- Can you stop controlling things and just go with the flow?

When I looked deeper inside myself, I understood that it had been my lack of self-love that caused me to hold myself back in life; it's what holds everyone back. I felt that I did not deserve prosperity, but I was not consciously aware of this until I began coaching and working with my subconscious. I didn't get it until I started feeling rather than thinking. I had to dig deep to see what the truth was. Was I peaceful? Was I happy? Was I fulfilled? Was I truthful and forthright in all my relationships? I always felt that my sense of humour helped me see the funny, light-hearted side of life but I was not peaceful. What was that anyway? I did not feel fulfilled and was not sure what my purpose was yet.

Everyone has a purpose; do you know what yours is?

Do you know what your soul is here to learn in this life?

What is your purpose? You are here for a reason.

Do you feel completely fulfilled in life?

I could have been told when I was a child that I hadn't eaten all of my dinner so as a result, I did not deserve any dessert. I unconsciously held onto this information and stored it away inside. Then I became an adult and was unable to attract what I desired because I felt somewhere inside I did not deserve it. I had been programmed, conditioned, brainwashed and hypnotized into believing I was not worthy and I didn't even know it.

This happens to everyone. I was an adult for a long time before I realized that when I went out to dinner, I would finish everything on my plate but didn't have to. Sometimes I didn't even like what I was eating but because I was trained as a kid to eat everything on my plate so not to leave any waste, it was automatic. One time I finally thought, 'Say what? I'm paying for this and if I don't like it, I don't have to eat it.' What a revelation.

I had grown up being a doer. I helped a lot around the house and took care of my siblings, always being there to work because I was the strong, capable oldest daughter. Once I began to work on my self- worth, I noticed that when I decided to take some time off, I would hear a little voice inside reminding me that I was not accomplishing anything and to get back to work again. This is hardly inner peace. I was not allowed to sleep in when growing up so, it is a challenge to do so as an adult; that's not loving. Even after I decided to meditate every day, if something else got in the way and I was unable to do so, I was hard on myself for missing it. This is not love.

Once I began to feel love for myself in every situation, I stopped judging myself, stopped being hard on myself and began treating myself as I would a child – with love and compassion. Every situation in our lives exists to give us an opportunity to practice self-love. I started giving myself permission to be gentle with myself in every way, every day. It was my inner child that I began to love again; that little girl inside me who was abandoned when I forgot to love myself. I forgot to love her. When I take care of my emotions, it is my inner child, or my little girl who I connect with again to feel my own self-love; she represents that to me.

Now, ask yourself these questions:

Are you pushing yourself to always do more without showing balance by taking time off?

Are you hard on yourself, putting yourself down sometimes or all the time?

Do you judge others? Do you also judge yourself?

Do you take care of yourself when you feel under the weather by showing your self-love, boosting your immune system, getting enough rest, eating healthy foods?

Are you numbing yourself by using drugs or alcohol? If so, what is it you don't want to feel?

Can you feel your inner child wanting attention and love from you?

Do you feel unloved by someone else? Maybe they are reflecting your own lack of love back to you. Others are our mirror so watch how they treat you and take responsibility, knowing you can improve your own behaviour by improving your self-worth.

you can do it too!

Practice this exercise to help you re-connect to your self- love:

CONNECTING TO YOUR SELF-WORTH

- Find a private place where you will not be disturbed. Lie down, close your eyes and breathe deeply, placing one hand on your solar plexus, just below your rib cage. This is where your emotions live and where you can imagine a Bridge between the worlds.

- Picture yourself on an imaginary Bridge which connects the two worlds; your world and the world of your inner child who is you when you were little.

- On the Bridge, notice the peace and beauty all around you. Feel the warmth of the sun; hear the birds singing and the wind blowing gently through your hair. This is calm and soothing and a place that you can come back to at anytime to feel safe and peaceful.

- As you walk on the Bridge notice yourself as a child walking closer to you and feel the excitement as you run into each other's arms, loving each other and hugging as you reconnect once again. Your child may be reluctant and stand back or shy, but whatever the reaction is, do not abandon your child; stay with them. Promise you will never leave your child again and that you will always be there loving them and parenting them. Feel yourself reconnecting and know that this is self-love you are once again feeling.

- When you do this exercise, you will no longer need anyone else to fill you up or give you love because you will have all

> the self-love inside you that you need. Practice this as often as you need to truly feel your self- worth and whenever any negative feelings come up for you.

How can an adult be free to prosper in life and love themselves if they have been fearful since childhood? Once in high school a group of friends and I rented a hotel room in Niagara Falls to have a party. We were excited about this fun weekend plan. I knew I could make my curfew of 11:00 and so did not tell my parents where I was going, but my soul had other plans for me. At some point that night we were dancing, drinking and having fun in our hotel room and the police came to the door raiding our party. They weren't there to tell us to be quiet because we were making too much noise or to tell us that someone had puked in the hallway and to clean it up; rather they were there because they said that they had received a phone call alerting them that we were doing a lot of drugs. For the next hour or so, the police had us take off our shoes so they could check for drugs hidden in the holes we had previously drilled into our heels. Say what? To us, it was ridiculous but we were sort of scared. After an hour of searching both us and the room high and low, the police told us why they were there and we put the story all together. Several strangers had tried to crash our party earlier in the evening but we had turned them away and they had called the police, lying about our intentions and our party. We were innocently accused and having fun doing nothing wrong, but I knew I had to go home and tell my parents the truth. I had not done anything immoral or inappropriate but because there had been police involved, and I had missed my curfew, I knew I was in big trouble. I hung my head, put my innocent seventeen year old tail between my legs and went home feeling guilty to face the monster that was my mother. My father probably agreed with her but she was always the one on the front lines who did the dirty work. I don't remember the details but she was not happy. I was always a good girl, honest and moral but I was so afraid of her wrath that I had worried, suffered and died a thousand deaths by the time I walked into the house that night. To actually be punished for this was so unnecessary because I'd already been in hell from the fear, way before I got home. That was my upbringing and that is fear. Love does not exist where there is fear; it's one or the other.

I began to look at other past experiences and question my behaviour. Why had I attracted a boyfriend who treated me disrespectfully? Fifteen years ago when I knew him, I would have told you that he was to blame because he was mean and bully-like a lot of the time. Now, however, I see him as a gift. In his treatment of me he was clearly reflecting my abuse of myself on some level as I did not take care of myself or did not listen to my body when it spoke to me about what it needed. I was distracted by the busyness of my life, but numbed myself with whatever I could at the time. And part of my mistreatment of myself was not being able to stand up to him and be authentic. I had not yet learned to listen to my body or soul; didn't know I was even on a journey. The realization that he was a sign showing me my lack of self-worth I now see as something positive; I just didn't get it then. People only treat you as badly as you let them.

Always remember that the universe is neutral and that every experience, relationship, person or incident that we attract into our lives is the mirror of something inside ourselves that the universe wants us to look at. Take responsibility and see the signs. Whatever someone is doing to you, you are doing to yourself and they are the reflection for you to learn by.

Taking responsibility for my own emotions has been a life-altering shift for me. Now, I would never say that someone has made me feel guilty for anything, because no one has control over my emotions. If I feel guilt, I have chosen to feel it and I take responsibility for owning my emotions because they are mine. Only I can do something about them and blaming someone else for my feelings is inappropriate.

A trigger occurs when there are unfelt emotions hidden in my body somewhere and someone does something to bug me, bringing up an old feeling that rises to the surface and leaks out. Remembering not to project that anger on others is important and there is an opportunity to heal that wound by feeling it when it rises to the surface. Unfelt emotions sit in our muscles and organs and are toxic, sometimes creating disease in the body. Every trigger I hold inside, I know began when I was a child and has become a habit because it is a wound that needs to be addressed. I learned this behaviour from my parents who modelled it and they learned it from theirs. We all hand down to the next generation our lack of self-worth because we don't know any better. We are the first generation who can make a difference by learning and applying these truths so that our children will grow up feeling their own self-love. Reconnect with your own self-worth to be authentic and help inspire others around you to do the same thing.

When we are feeling uncomfortable emotions, we can practice tapping into our self-worth by going to the Bridge and releasing that emotion so that we can have space again to fill up with our own self-love.

RELEASING

- Picture yourself on the Bridge and reconnect with the feelings of peace and beauty that is all around you in this special place.

- Find your little girl or boy and hug and love them. This will reconnect you with your feelings of love for them and reconnect you to your own self-love at the same time.

- Bring anyone onto the Bridge that you want to be honest with, want to heal with or feel the need to tell how they have hurt you. Speak your truth and tell them how you feel. Whatever it is, feel it fully and let your child speak through your emotions. Hit a pillow and curse and swear if you are angry to get it out of your body. If you are sad, then feel it and tell them. Own your emotions and feel them to release them. The person only has to be there energetically – if you see them in your imagination, they are with you. You can also do this with people who are deceased and heal your relationship with them by talking to them and releasing the stored emotions.

- As you release these low vibration feelings from your body, you will feel lighter and have more space inside to fill up with your own self-love. You are reconnecting to your source.

- Practice this exercise as often as you need to release and love yourself again. Your sense of self-worth improves every time you do this.

Going onto the Bridge to feel the love for your inner little girl or boy is only one of the ways that we can practice reconnecting to our self-worth. Meditation helps me feel calm, joyful and happy and is a very effective way to combat the stressful effects of everyday life and the busy world we live in. This inner peace that is created by meditating is not momentary but also affects me throughout the day by providing me with the coping skills I need to avoid being reactive, to stay centred and feel my source. It raises both emotional and physical energy and helps me shift to a positive, high vibration when I feel challenged. It helps release tension and anxiety, reenergizes me and also improves my health by helping to strengthen my immune system.

The emotions of love, joy, kindness, empathy and gratitude have a high vibration and can contribute to our sense of self-worth when we are feeling them. Having fresh flowers at home reminds me of the beauty of nature and brings me back to myself as I enjoy them in both my work space and my sacred space. Being kind to someone – a stranger on the street – with some small gesture or even smiling at people can be a kindness and help raise our vibration and that of the recipient as well.

Can you perform a random act of kindness for someone else each day? If you do, you will feel inner peace and love and help raise their vibration as well.

When we receive positive energy back from someone, it's like giving a hug and when we feel grateful, it is a powerful, positive sentiment.

I decided to train myself by writing five things daily that I was grateful for. After doing this for a while, it became a habit for me and I automatically stop myself now during my day and thank God and the angels for the little things that surround me in the moment; a sharp pencil, the sky, beautiful weather, someone's laugh or even hearing a song I love. This also helps me to be present, feel happy to be alive and helps shift my energy towards positivity or helps keep it there. Singing and laughing are two of the fastest ways to raise your vibration and feel joy. There is always joy in laughter and it is a gift for me to know that whenever I laugh with someone, or make them laugh, we are connected and happy.

Can you write down five things that you are grateful for every day? A shift will occur to create positive energy for you.

Forgiveness helps us return to self-love and is more important for the person doing the forgiving than the other person. We are on earth in this lifetime to learn forgiveness and Neal Donald Walsch wrote *The Little Soul and the Sun*, (Hampton Roads Publishing Company, Inc., 1998) which illustrates this journey beautifully in a children's book. I often read this book to friends and clients and it's difficult not to cry when hearing the story as it helps everyone reconnect with a sense of self-worth through its wisdom and truth. Walsch tells the story of two souls who are friends in heaven and one soul promises the other to do something hurtful to him when they are on earth so that his friend can have an opportunity to forgive him. When he does this terrible thing, the hurtful soul asks his friend to remember who he is and that he is doing this thing as a gift. So, both little souls come forth into a new lifetime and wait anxiously to be able to experience one another as Hurtful and the other as Forgiveness. This wonderful story helps illustrate how we can forgive those who we feel have hurt us in some way by showing us that they are really our soul friends and that we have a soul contract with them. We can forgive because we know that we have hurt others too and that God has sent us only angels. It's impossible to read this book and not think of someone who we have not yet forgiven so we can remember that it is never too late to do this and feel our self-worth.

Is there anyone in your life who you have not forgiven for something they've done? It's never too late to forgive and free yourself of that pain you've been holding inside which holds you back from true peace and love.

Adults usually have a bully in their lives. For me, this is someone that makes me feel that I want to walk on eggshells around them because they usually react in anger. A bully projects that anger on everyone in their vicinity and I tend to not want to rattle their cage, so in the past I have become the mouse hoping they will not erupt. Do you recognize this feeling? I have dealt with people in positions of power, a boss, a department head and administrators who I answered to in various jobs that have taken their power to this place and alienated everyone around them. This can be especially difficult for people lacking self-worth because their fear causes them to use the excuse of being afraid to lose their job if they speak up. So, we tend to stay away and avoid our authentic feelings. Great leaders know that people respond to appreciation and love rather than criticism and anger. This starts when we are children and won't stop when we become adults until we heal that part of us that is afraid to stand up to the bully. We have given away our power by being a victim. I hear people use the excuse that they won't talk to the bully because it won't do any good or they say that the bully won't change, so why bother? The truth is that people are afraid and it isn't about changing anyone else because that is impossible. It's about us standing up to the bully and speaking from our hearts. This garners us courage. I believe that all humans are not born being courageous but rather when we go to the fire, we learn this lesson. Once it's learned, none of us will attract or be triggered by a bully again.

Do you have someone in your life you are afraid to be honest with and feel bullied by? Take them on the Bridge and stand up to them to speak your truth to release your fear and leave space for your self-worth. Then, be brave and do it in real life, this time from your heart.

My parents would have believed that in order to keep nine children in line they needed to control things, and they did just that. Instead, what they needed to be was organized and compassionate. Control is rigid and does not allow for openness, flexibility or ease. My parents modelled control so I too became controlling. I would write lists of things to do because I did not have much of a short term memory and was brain-fogged and I thought it would help me feel more organized when I accomplished them. However, this would also give me an opportunity to berate myself and be hard on myself when I did not get everything on the list done that day. So, I worked hard at letting go of control by beginning to see that what I got done was perfect and what did not get done could wait until another day. This way is more peaceful and includes the belief that the universe is supporting me and that everything that is important and essential will get done, as it always does. The rest can wait and I needed to trust in this truth.

Is there anything that you can stop controlling in your life? Is there anyone you ask to do something for you and then you are triggered when you see that it isn't done your way? Can you be flexible around this issue when they do it their way? Can you go with the flow? If not, why not?

Many adults think that because they are confident and have grown up, that they have a sense of self-worth but it doesn't just happen to us that way. I know when I see people afraid to speak their truth, who feel bullied and who live in fear that it is their lack of self-love holding them back; but they usually don't know this. It's clear to me because I lived in that place for so long and I recognize it having made the great escape to self-worth. We all look at our children and youth and see that they need help with their self-worth but unless we restore ours as parents, teachers and guides, we will never be able to really help them. Even the wealthiest people in the world can't buy self-worth. It's inside us and only we can do the work to restore it. That is why we are on earth and it is everyone's journey to come back to their own self-love.

If you haven't started to do the work yet, it's never too late. Love yourself again by remembering who you really are.

7. reaching back for help

Each soul or entity will and does return,–Life is continuous.

-Edgar Cayce

The concept of reincarnation is a philosophical and religious one that explains that our soul journeys from lifetime to lifetime and we return in order to learn lessons. Much research in this area has come from the field of hypnosis and there is a great belief in exploring reincarnation as a valuable way to heal. I now know this to be true because I have been helped in this way.

I also know that anyone who does the research will see that there is no other answer than that we do come back because there are only so many souls, so when our physical body dies, we return again to earth school. Eventually, it will be no longer necessary for a soul to re-enter a body because they will be enlightened enough to stay behind in heaven.

Past life therapy explains why it is important for us to be responsible for our behaviour and that all the information we need to heal is contained within our subconscious mind. I know that my soul has brought trauma from other lives and I have returned there to work on healing. It has been an extraordinary and helpful experience to do so.

I believe now that we create our own illnesses and that even the common cold has its beginning in some emotion that has a message for us to learn from. This was a concept that I heard about when I first began my journey to wellness and it ignited my curiosity.

How could I have been the creator of my own illness?

The power of this belief system which I later adopted helped me take responsibility for my health but also helped me understand that spiritual messages can manifest as health issues from past lifetimes. Sometimes we have unfinished business, lessons still not learned or the trauma of a tragic death that we can bring into our next life and which can impact our physical, mental and emotional well-being.

I did have questions:

- Was I born with this illness in my body, or did it develop later?
- Why was it taking me so long to heal from chronic fatigue and Candida when other people heal from these conditions in only months?

- What did I still have to learn to get better?

So much healing had taken place in my life already but I still felt a need to approach my journey on a holistic basis. It was time for me to discover the truth of where my soul had been and to heal those wounds that had left me scarred from past lives. I was about to unlock the secret of why my life had been so difficult and why I had been blocking and holding myself back, suffering sickness.

Through coaching I looked back into my previous life hoping to discover the reason for these health issues. The results of this helped me understand, learn lessons, let go, heal and move forward. Colleen remembered my most recent past life, having been with me, and was able to guide me back there to heal my body, heart and soul.

Usually when past lives are visited, hypnosis is used as a regression technique, but in coaching sessions we used the power of our intention to access our subconscious and have our soul's revisit the Concentration Camp where as a woman I had spent a very painful part of my most recent past life. Returning to the trauma experienced there was horrific. I could see that I had brought the effects of PTSD (Post Traumatic Stress Disorder) into this lifetime with me in my soul's memory of the devastating treatment I suffered there. In the Camps, I watched as my three children were taken away from me; I was separated from them to do hard labour. Eventually all of us were sent to the gas chamber. I know now the depth of the pain and what that does to a soul, to a body, to a spirit, as the tragedy of it has been carried in my broken heart from that lifetime into this one.

The first time I revisited that life again, it was so real that I was still feeling those memories for a week after. I knew I was ready for my soul and I to travel back there again and that I had been guided to this place to recall and heal, but it didn't make it easy to face. Life there was beyond brutal. There were beatings, rape and sometimes we would connect with the guards in order to stay alive. For a while in one camp I was lucky to secure a position inside tailoring uniforms and this prolonged my life which could easily have been snuffed out quickly doing hard labour outside. In another camp we were exposed to the elements in the winter with no gloves, outerwear or even shoes. And, there was very little food, if any, when we returned to camp at the end of each day.

After my first regression, Colleen would call me every few days and ask me how I was doing and I would respond in confusion. I was still 'in it' and she would encourage me to just feel those feelings and remember the memories to heal the wounds that now were open again. This was my first time going back into my past life and it was painful but it wouldn't be the last time I had to revisit that hell; I've been there many, many times since.

Do you have any weird or unusual dreams that bring up deep, fearful feelings? It could be a past life experience that is triggering your dreams for you to remember and heal.

Children often remember previous lives. Do you remember living in another time?

Children often have birthmarks and/or birth defects from a previous life and recall being killed or wounded. Do you have any birthmarks that you attribute to a past life?

I lost other children too, but the most devastating for me was saying good-bye to my six year old son who I still see clearly in my memory today in a barracks in the camp. As he holds the hand of some adult who has promised to take care of him, he is taken away and as I watch him, I register the wool cap he wears and hope that the little jacket he has on will keep him warm in the coming winter months; but I know it won't. He is being led away and looks back at me with sad, fearful, confused brown eyes as we say good-bye. The image is painfully tattooed on my soul forever. I see it clearly and feel the intensity of the pain of what it is like to lose my child. He was disabled in some way and that accounts for some of the additional guilt I have felt throughout this lifetime because I could not protect or save him. This has been the most crushing loss to me ever and I continue to work on healing this wound because it is deep. I know this is why I chose to come into a family with seven brothers, so that I could nurture and help take care of them. I loved being around those little boys who were my brothers and they have helped me also heal this loss.

A few years ago, I was driving up Yonge Street in Toronto and noticed a little boy walking from the drug store with a large piece of Bristol board, probably for a class project. As I saw the wind pick up, I felt something as I watched him and in that split second I began to cry. Then, I did not remember but later reflecting, I understood that I had been triggered by seeing him and this brought up the memory of my six year old son exterminated in the Concentration Camp. I also remembered that Mother's Day was a week away and that that holiday was exposing old wounds unhealed from my unconscious. Although the pain is raw and deep, I am grateful to have the exercise of going to the Bridge to feel that hurt and let it go. No one knows how long it will take or how many times I will have to remember his little face looking back at me as he says good-bye for the last time. I just keep going there to heal that trauma by feeling it and being in the energy of that loss fully.

I also began to recognize past life trauma in others around me as I learned about my own. While teaching college, one of my students was in her twenties and looking forward to getting married and having children. She was however, desperately afraid of the birthing experience and approached me about this. It was evident to me that she either died during childbirth or experienced some kind of trauma while giving birth in another life. We talked about how she could move forward to heal this through the help of hypnosis and coaching and she felt better having more knowledge and understanding of it. This quite often is enough to heal that wound and release the pain.

For many years I have been working on healing this past life experience in the Camps and sometimes answers I'm looking for come through my dreams.

The explanation as to why I had often felt claustrophobic was something I wanted to explore. I can remember a difficult experience when I was visiting the CN Tower in Toronto one summer and in order to get to the top, I was squeezed into a tiny elevator that was not air-conditioned and became hotter as it moved up the side of the Tower. I recall feeling so uncomfortable with the heat and the lack of air that it created panic in me; I felt like I could not breathe. One breath of fresh air would have helped as I felt like I was dying and being smothered. It was not a long trip up the side of the Tower but to me, it seemed to go on forever. I realize now that it was a soul memory of a death experience from the Camps and the answer came one night in a dream. I was in the Concentration Camp, inside the gas chamber with my back to the large metal door that held us in. I can hear it being slammed shut behind me because I am the last one in. I am surrounded by many other people who suddenly realize that we were all about to be exterminated as the gas began to seep in and everyone felt the terror of this truth. People began screaming as they scramble over each other to get to the door and out, trying to change their inevitable fate. I still feel the hard metal of it against my back where I was pinned and crushed under the weight of the others who tried desperately to be released from their deaths. I see this vision as I write these words and know that it is the reason for that feeling of claustrophobia, darkness and the inability to breathe that has affected me at times in my life when put into close, dark, hot spaces. To heal this, I learned to slow down, remind myself to breathe and remember that God is there too; not just in the positive in life, but also there in the chaos and my death in the Concentration Camp and this helps me to feel peace. I continue to be open to feel that pain of that trauma fully to heal it as my soul remembers and I move forward in life.

The deep sense of peace and healing that I arrived at by remembering my past was helping improve my self-worth and making a difference in my life. I was no longer in victim mode; I was looking better than I ever had before and people noticed and commented. I was able to speak my truth, be authentic and stand up to the bully. And, I was always taking care of my emotional body daily, checking in with my feelings. I was feeling pretty good about the process and at the end of working with Colleen for a couple of years I took her Coaching Certification Course and became a Life Coach so I too could help other people improve their lives by restoring their own self-worth. I will continue to help those who find their way to me to ask questions about life and how to improve it and I find myself coaching people all day, every day as I bring the truth to remind them of the work that we all need to do.

I also continue to practice on the Bridge and will always teach and use this exercise to help feel a sense of self–worth. An opportunity arose that provided me with a chance to utilize my learning when presented with a situation in the apartment where I had moved after my car accident.

A lot of noise was occurring around me and the couple who lived next door often fought, which left me feeling anxious and upset. I would be awakened in the night hearing their loud verbal disputes and not be able to get back to sleep. There were other instances of noise also with neighbours upstairs leaving their television on all night above my bedroom. It was disturbing. Because I was on the ground floor, people walking by coming from the bars, drunk and loud, as they passed my apartment did not seem to bother me as much; I'd just drop off back to sleep. When there was a fight or anger, however, I seemed deeply affected by it. My heart would pound, my breathing became shallow and I would not be able to go back to sleep again.

- Why was this happening to me and why was it so upsetting?
- Why was I able to go back to sleep immediately if there was no violence involved?

- Why was I attracting so much noise constantly anyway?

I did everything I knew how to face this issue but nothing was changing, and I was clear to me that there was a message in this sign that I needed to heal. Something was calling me deeper into the subconscious – something I had to address. I decided to see a Consulting Hypnotist and booked a Past Life Regression session because I knew it was a past life trauma that I needed to examine. At my appointment my hypnotist explained hypnosis to me and used a soft, gentle voice to help transport me back through the blue mist into a placeless time in a timeless place to another lifetime. I enjoyed the feeling of floating, landing firmly on the ground and I was encouraged to look at my feet and describe what was on them, if anything. As I saw myself in a past life, I was a blonde man with long hair and I wore a brown leather fabric tunic and loose, leather-wrapped sandals on my feet. My head was protected with a metal helmet and I had a metal breastplate and shield and a short dagger-like knife; I was a Viking warrior. The scene I describe is one where I was standing atop a hill overlooking a battlefield during a time of war. I still see it clearly and there is chaos and destruction all around me. I smell the odour of burning and see that the thatched roofs of the houses in our village are on fire and I hear the screams and moaning of people on the battlefield below me as they are wounded and lie dying. I was a man who was honoured with a title or award in my village; I was highly respected and sought after for advice, and had a positive reputation for being a good man who cared about and wanted to help and protect others. To see this destruction was very difficult for me.

Still in hypnosis, I was later taken to the death experience and I found myself back on the same battlefield. Because you detach from any physical or emotional pain during hypnosis, I was able to describe my death as I viewed it while my soul left my body. As I slowly walked from the hill top where I had been standing, I entered the battlefield below as a confident, veteran Viking warrior. It came as completely unexpected when I was suddenly, shockingly impaled with a sword which pierced by body, entering through my back and exiting through my ribcage. I had felt strong, protected and assured, having been in battles many times before. This was so unanticipated and for some reason I was caught off guard with no warning that it was about to happen and it made the sudden blow even more traumatic for me. As I lay on the battlefield with my life's energy running out of me, chaos was all around and the smells of blood, smoke and fire along with the sound of the cries and moans of other people who were also wounded or dying – that is my painful recollection. Hearing horse's hooves running, trampling me as I lay forgotten and dying on the battlefield along with the sounds of death surrounding me left an indelible mark on my soul as I hear and see it now. My hypnotist gently guided me back through the blue mist and as I floated between lifetimes again, I was guided to stop at another previous life to further heal.

This time I landed back on earth and was a woman with bare feet and I was in a very dark place. I was wearing rags, surrounded by blackness and I was on the floor scrubbing it with raw, red, wet, painful and freezing cold hands. I recognized this place; I was imprisoned and commented that I had visited many times before. I was back in the Concentration Camp, working hard to stay alive. There is a great presence of authority around me that is a big, threatening, mean, angry energy. I am in fear and trying to do a good job so that I don't get into trouble and can stay alive. Everyone around me is also emotionally raw because we feel death close by and we fear our captors. People are afraid and although we all want to help and support each other it doesn't happen. I want everyone to be quiet so I can find some peace. The fear is intense and the noise makes it worse when I am constantly hearing gunshots and stomping boots from the guards coming towards me. It's dark. There is no light. Its hell and I just want it to be quiet because I need to find some peace.

In this place, constantly hearing pain along with feeling my own is difficult because the suffering surrounding me is intense. I just want everyone to be quiet so I can get some sleep. The only peace I am able to find is when I do sleep and even if I have nightmares, it is more peaceful than being awake and experiencing the incessant weeping of people in so much pain, disease, fear and sickness. I have a close friend there and it is Colleen. We both had a deeper understanding of what was going on around us and we tried to help people deal with their fear. She helped everyone she came into contact with because of her deep sense of love.

I wonder what keeps me going because I want peace so much that part of me wants to die to feel it again. I am in small quarters and the smells, cries and anguish are impossible to shut out; there is no relief from it. As my hypnotist guided me to the death experience I once again recognized where I was as I had been there before in a dream. We were in the gas chamber and we were about to die. I am at the door and people were weeping and sobbing as they realized what was happening and they clamoured trying to get out, crushing me. There is no air. The sound I'm hearing is an air raid siren and the screaming and crying becomes quieter as people begin to die and find some peace once again. I am able to tell you this story because

I lived longer than the others. While I was watching them die, I remember thinking at one point, 'Why am I still alive? Am I ever going to die?' Everyone else was dead and I was still there, waiting and watching this tragedy unfold. I know now that I promised the others in a soul contract to do this so that they would not have to die alone. I also realized then that I had fought to stay alive longer so that I could experience their deaths before mine because I wanted to make sure that their souls left their bodies first. I wanted to know for certain that they were all on their way to heaven before I went. I promised to wait for them to die so they would not feel alone in the death experience; I'd go last and that is what happened. I didn't mind because I felt their souls once again at peace and no longer in such pain after they passed on.

Over the years, while I was struggling with my health and the environment, I had always been sensitive to scents and odours which invaded my body, assaulting me. When a student would come into my classroom wearing perfume, I felt vulnerable because I was unable to get away from it and it immediately made me sick, headachey and nauseated. When I was a Viking and lay dying on the battlefield, the intense smell of death, the burning houses around me and the smell of blood where I fell had also impacted me, leaving a soul memory that was indelible. In the Camps, hearing the pain and suffering of others and the smell of death were constants.

As I reintegrated myself back into the present, I understood that in both cases, I was surrounded by many people and lots of noise and smells during the death experience. I was also surrounded by other people suffering and constantly hearing this was traumatic. I held onto that stress on a soul level and brought it into this lifetime.

After bringing back the learning from this Hypnosis session, I understood the power of it as it helped me heal my noise issues. After that, whenever I would hear angry people fighting next door or drunken people pass by my apartment late at night, I would reassure myself that I was in this lifetime, not in the past, that I was safe and not dying. Then I would drop off to sleep again and be able to resume the peace I had felt earlier. This only needed to happen a couple of times and I believe it was healed. Interestingly, the noise that had been both upstairs and beside me from fighting couples suddenly stopped as well. This is how when we understand the source of our past life experience it can be healing especially when you have the courage to face whatever your soul guides you to.

After my positive experience of Past Life Regression through Hypnosis, I felt it was a way that I could help others heal too, so I decided to become a Consulting Hypnotist. Past Life Regression became a new passion for me. I became a Consulting Hypnotist and after that, a specialist in Past Life Regression. I felt strongly that this was going to blend beautifully with my Life Coaching and I would be able to build a business helping people using these combined modalities but again, my soul had other plans for me.

Nancy Newman

Everyone experiences past life memories but often they don't realize it:

Have you ever met anyone who felt immediately familiar to you?

Have you ever had a déjà vu experience where you were sure that you had experienced a scene or situation before?

Have you ever had weird dreams or nightmares of some incident that leaves you feeling emotional?

Have you ever had a recurring dream about something and don't know why?

The trauma suffered in lives already lived is often the basis of the suffering we again experience in the life we are presently living. Past life therapy opens up a door to heal by acknowledging and understanding the source of this pain. The benefits are evident when peace and harmony are restored after the trauma has been recalled, felt and understood. Regression therapy touched the deepest part of my soul and once I remembered what happened back then, I have been able to heal myself through love, acceptance and understanding. If you have the courage to go there and face your past to heal, your life will change as you allow more light to enter where that darkness has been inside your soul. It's awesome work.

You can do it, just like I did.

8. slipping back

Your soul knows the destiny of your journey. It will take you where you need to go.

-John O'Donohue

I had never known how to listen to my soul and it had been speaking to me my entire life. I didn't know how to hear it. Eventually, my life fell apart when I realized my health was shot because I had been ignoring its guidance; I just didn't get it yet.

Maybe I had given up listening when I was a child at the same time my sense of self–worth vanished. But, I certainly hear it now and I know my soul is the voice inside speaking to me through my intuition, my creativity, my passion, my imagination and my emotions.

The soul is not the voice of worry, thinking or trying to figure things out; that's the ego which is much louder and the soul which speaks quietly is often overpowered by it. The soul has feminine energy and has a feminine voice. As I began to take care of myself more lovingly, I was more able to listen for its gentleness as it showed me the way forward.

When I am in my heart it's easy to hear my soul and you too can hear yours when you truly feel your gentleness. Just listen between the space in your breath and in the silence of your day; just listen when you are being creative or feeling passionate about something; your soul is there too, speaking to you, guiding you. As you begin to trust your intuition you will discover your ability to connect with and listen to your soul.

My soul understood that I was willing to go wherever I needed to in order to heal and I was determined to know the truth. This decision seemed to unhinge the portal to my previous lifetimes. I began to slip back into past lives easily like a door that opens and closes with the gentle breeze of my desire to be better. I had been visiting the Concentration Camp often and once I became a Consulting Hypnotist, practiced self-hypnosis along with being hypnotized by others, going deeper to remember became easy. Comfortable with the familiarity of being in previous lives, I have continued working with my subconscious as guided by my soul. I carried on going back to remember and release the trauma there.

Being triggered by something that ignites a soul memory has become a regular part of my life as I react to the emotions I once knew and slip back into that lifetime. Movies, books, nightmares and dreams can act as conduits to my past and I believe you too, may experience this and might not realize it. When this happens to me, a part of my consciousness is transported back to that lifetime and I co-exist in both dimensions simultaneously. When I have a nightmare of being raped and I am dying at the hands of my captors, it means that the fear of that experience is still in my body brought to present day through my soul's memory. My soul knows I want to heal and free myself of this painful trauma and the only way I can do this is to feel that fear, so I continue to do so to heal old wounds.

Have you ever thought about why you are drawn to a certain kind of movie or book? What drives your desire to find out more about certain concepts or periods in history? It could be a previous life that is pulling you back to heal some aspect of it.

The best time of the day for me to hear my soul's voice is late at night or early in the morning. When I first wake up if I have any questions or am looking for ideas for help with some creative project, I ask my soul. The answer comes quickly, clearly and is always an awesome one. You too can practice this exercise to get better at listening and improve your creative problem solving skills.

I began to realize that I was slipping back into a previous life when I spent weeks at a time remembering my experiences there. I travelled back to the Concentration Camp so often and finally understood that events were also triggering me back into other multiple past lives.

I had given my soul permission to take me there because I needed to heal. When this happens, the symptoms that I experience are subtle enough that I can go about my daily life and work but part of me just feels out of it. I feel confused and a bit spacey and like my consciousness has left my body because my awareness is in two lifetimes at once; here and back there and it breaks up my ability to totally be present. My appetite diminishes to nearly nothing and only small amounts of soft, cooked food are what my body can handle. This is probably because my energy is needed to deal with the emotions of being in two lives at once and not the digestion process. I don't sleep particularly well, but it doesn't seem to matter and the feelings and visions that I receive help me also revisit the pain of being back there. While my soul shows me the memories I need to be with, I am still in the experience.

This has continued to happen to me for many years. My appetite returning is usually a good sign that I am coming out of the experience and I feel my consciousness drop back into my body. This can last up to three weeks. It is a time to work on myself and just lay low in life as I recall and feel.

Do you ever feel out of it and confused and have memories from another time? If you do, just be with the feelings because you are healing by being in that space.

The Messengers, by Julia Ingram and G. W. Hardin (Pocket Star Publishing, 1998) is a book that I was guided to buy, I thought, because of the beautiful angel on its cover. This is a true story about the life of a Portland, Oregon business man who with the help of angels, understood that he was the reincarnation of Paul the Apostle and walked alongside Jesus, 2000 years ago. As he works with a Consulting Hypnotist who regresses him, he recalls his growing friendship with Jesus and also explains the message that Jesus was teaching the people as He travelled around preaching so long ago.

After I finally reached the end of the book one night, I slept and got out of bed the next morning, walked a few steps, suddenly felt nauseated and was aware of something that came over me like a wave of energy. I realized I was being triggered into that past lifetime by *The Messengers* because I had been there with Jesus when He was on earth. I was not only a follower but also one of His disciples and my deep emotions of that life transported me back there to be with St. Paul and Jesus. I remembered my life as a disciple; Colleen was there too and remembers. I was guided by my angels who told me I would not sleep that night but that I would be fine. I was unable to eat much food beyond water and protein shakes throughout this experience which lasted several weeks. Part of me was there and part of me was here. This also helped me remember that I did not want to come into this lifetime because I did not want to leave God and heaven.

I also now understood that the work we do through Life Coaching, helping people restore their self-worth came from this past life when I was on earth with Jesus. It was the same work He did, preached and taught the people.

When Colleen was writing her book, *Pocket Guide to Your Heart*, I was working on the illustrations she wanted me to do for it. During our first meeting, we began by reading her manuscript and twenty pages into the first chapter, she was telling a story of a time when she had fallen off her bike, hit her head on a rock and went home with blood running down her face. I felt something shift in me almost like a click while reading but I didn't process it right then. When I was teaching a few days later at the Academy of Design, I was giving direction to my students at the beginning of class and I suddenly realized I had blood running down my face; my nose was bleeding badly. It happened so quickly that there was no warning and my students gasped at its onset. When I put my hand up to my face, I saw it was covered with blood as if I had been bleeding for hours. I gave my students work to do and went to the washroom to stop the flow and clean up; or so I thought. That didn't happen. I tried everything I knew to stop the blood, but nothing worked. There was something very different about this nosebleed because nothing even slowed down the flow. It kept bleeding like crazy. I couldn't spend the day in the washroom and had to go back to class, so I stuffed my nose with Kleenex but had to leave class again every few minutes to replace the bloody, saturated sponges that were now keeping the blood from running down my face. I finally made it to the break, half way through my three hour class and gave my students fifteen minutes off before we re-convened. I went downstairs to the drug store for help from the pharmacist, a little panicked at this point. Nothing I had ever experienced about nosebleeds was helping in this situation.

The pharmacist suggested a couple of things that everyone knows not to do to stop a bloody nose, so he was no help. I went back to class, my skin colour now grey as the life drained from me along with what seemed to be every ounce of my life's blood and all I could do was to sit down in the corner of my classroom with my head back so I didn't flood the floor. I was worried; this was very unusual and I knew it was happening to get my attention, but for what? I apologized to my students for the inconvenience, but they worked away on their assignments for the day, always gracious and supportive as well as being concerned for me. I tried to help them on their work every few minutes but was mostly dealing with my nose and the blood. What the hell was going on here, anyway?

At this point, I gave in and decided to go to the hospital after class was over in an hour. I needed help; this was now scary. I was constantly in and out of the bathroom, grabbing more toilet paper to shove up my nose when I was standing in a stall across from my classroom for the fiftieth time in two hours, at my wit's end. I was sure I had to learn something here so I could finally stop bleeding and go back to class. I begged my angels to tell me what I needed to know.

Clairvoyantly, they showed me that it was related to my mother's death many years ago. The shock I felt when I realized she was dying was traumatic. At the time, my mother had been in the hospital having a liver biopsy and I went to visit her. It was my understanding that it was a pretty routine procedure but when I walked into her room, I was suddenly overwhelmed by the feeling that she was dying. My youngest brother was only six and there were eight other siblings besides me to take care of. What were we going to do without a mother? The shock of this was too much to bear and I suddenly felt nauseous. After quickly saying hi to her, I left her room, found the closest door and ran downstairs and outside where I could finally breathe again. After a little while, I composed myself and returned to visit with her. Maybe my mother had also just realized that she was close to death and I empathically picked up on that feeling. No one else in my family knew this truth yet, and realizing it was a blow to my emotional state as it would be to anyone's. I had clearly buried it because at the time I had a lot to do knowing my mother was dying. These feelings about her death had now risen to the surface of my consciousness as I slipped back remembering, triggered by hearing about Colleen's accident. They were now present and on the surface so I could also be with them and feel and release what I had buried so long ago. But back to the bleeding nose and getting it stopped.

Although I had decided to go to the hospital as soon as class ended, I was concerned about how they would treat my nosebleed. I knew now that the blood was from an early life emotional trauma and wanted to deal with it myself. So, I told my angels that I finally understood what was happening but that if the bleeding didn't stop in the next 20 minutes, I was going to Emergency because I had had enough. And, it stopped. Because I now knew the source of the trigger and understood I needed to go to the pain and shock around my mother's death, the attention-getting blood stopped.

Later, I spent time remembering the death of my mother and how it had impacted my life and the lives of everyone in my family when she left us. This was good to have my feelings on the surface again so I could heal this traumatic event. I had several of the same kind of nosebleeds over the next few months but at least I knew why they were happening and they were less severe. Interestingly enough, it never occurred when I was home and could easily take care of it. It always happened when I was in a public place or classroom or in the car and somewhere where I felt helpless, vulnerable and exposed and where the pressure was on to get to its source. I knew I had to do more healing until they were gone completely.

Another unconscious return to a past trauma occurred on a day when I was at my part-time job selling furniture and my friend and manager, Marcia Sanchez, asked me how I saw my future unfolding. I confidently began to talk about my plans to teach high school again which I had recently decided to do after meeting a teacher who had been a colleague years ago. I decided that all my experience from being a working artist, entrepreneur, Life Coach and Consulting Hypnotist may be appreciated by a Board of Education and that my path seemed to be leading me back to the classroom. As we talked I was enjoying our easy, casual conversation about my plans but I realized in a minute that I began to feel my left foot hurt. As I continued talking over the next few minutes my foot quickly swelled up and became extremely painful. I stopped the conversation as I realized what was happening, showing Marcia that my foot was swollen and throbbing and that it started when we began talking about me going back to teaching; I knew it must be fear. I also knew there was something significant happening here and in a few minutes the excruciating pain confirmed to me that it was a sign. Our feet move us forward in life and I knew that my unconscious fears about teaching again were coming through because I suddenly could not walk or even stand.

Every illness has an emotional beginning; in less than five minutes I showed my friend how my football-sized foot had reflected my inner fear and we both watched, shocked at its immediate intensity. It was fairly close to the end of the day and there was no way I would have been able to take a streetcar or subway home; I couldn't even stand. Another friend helped carry me to a waiting taxi that would take me home and I felt confident that once I got there, I could heal this.

As the taxi dropped me off at home twenty minutes later, I had to hop to my apartment around my garden fence which took me ten minutes instead of two. The first thing I did was leave a message for my friend and trainer, Alex Savva, to cancel my appointment to train in the morning at his gym, CircuitFit. I said that I couldn't stand on my foot; it was in bad shape but that I would explain what happened when I saw him. Then I went to work. I went to the fear that I knew was there in my subconscious, and I felt it fully.

Years ago, when I left teaching, I swore that I would never go back because part of me really thought that I was sick because of the job. This belief was still held in my body and had just manifested itself in my inability to move forward because of my lame foot; it was a sign. My soul was showing me that I held that old fear of that old job in me and I believed it was the reason I got sick, but that wasn't true. I understood now that this old belief was unfounded because when I had decided to leave teaching almost twenty years previously, the decision was made from a place of illness. It hadn't been the job at all that made me sick. I knew now that it had been the trauma of my past life, the trauma I'd gone through as a child and my inability to take care of myself.

I went to the fear and I felt every bit of the anxiety that came up. I realized I was afraid to sit on the 401 every day on my way home from school and fall asleep in my car as I had so many years before because of my exhaustion. I was afraid of getting sick again if I went back there because it represented that ill period of my life to me; I had come so far. I stayed with it for a while. Having arrived home at 6:00, I just felt all the fear and cried and panicked until I was spent and the fear was gone. At 10:00 that night, my phone rang and I was able to run to answer it; actually run. My foot was completely healed. I could still feel the bruise in my cells of it having been there but I could walk again and the swelling was completely gone. The pain and swelling disappeared quickly once I started to feel my emotional pain and it healed. We heal ourselves. This is a perfect example to illustrate that every illness has its roots in our emotions.

The next morning I got up early and ran a mile to work out and touch base with Alex, who was shocked to see me after the message I had left the night before. I told him what had happened and how I had healed myself by going to the source, the emotions and fear around the changes I saw coming. Always supportive and willing to help me, he listened intently and commented that I must feel empowered by this practice as its effect was evident after this experience. It is empowering to know that we can heal ourselves by going to the source of the emotional pain.

Does this ever happen to you? Does your body suddenly hurt or do you get a pain and wonder why it appeared out of nowhere? If so, think back about what you were talking about or thinking just before it happened. That is the source of an unconscious fear that has been hiding in your body. Go to it, feel it to heal that part of you that is afraid.

Do you presently suffer from anything which causes you pain in some area of your body? If you are having pain in your feet for example, you are probably holding on to some anger around a relationship you have and someone you have not yet forgiven. Often we feel guilty about saying anything against a spouse or verbalizing that we are disappointed in them, but letting go of these negative feelings can heal our feet and our hearts; being honest with ourselves is the key.

Being able to see and experience my life and death from past lives including those lived hundreds and thousands of years ago has really been a life-changing experience. I have been helped as I live the healing and know the truth of who I am while I see the lessons in each lifetime.

Looking back, I would never have written the story of my life the way it has unfolded because I was setting my course along with the help of my ego and I was under the impression that I could call the shots. I know now it's not up to us to try and figure out our next move through life but rather to listen to the guidance of our soul because our soul knows. I am so happy to have my soul as a guide now and recognize and acknowledge it. I am able to listen to the voice that shows me the way because now I understand that my soul is with me always and speaking to me. Being able to visit previous lives so often has helped me immeasurably to clear out old pain and trauma from the wounds I have suffered so long ago in my past. It's a gift and I am grateful to be guided in this way.

9. surrender

It doesn't take a lot of strength to hang on. It takes a lot of strength to let go.

-J. C. Watts

Some people are confused when you tell them that to surrender is a good thing; they think it is the same as giving up.

Spiritual surrender means living in peace every day and letting go of what it is we are fighting so hard to hold onto. Some call it "surrender to win". I had been brought up with the belief that I would never get anywhere in life without hard work and I learned from my parents to control things. I thought that if I was trying to make something happen and it wasn't, that I should keep trying and never quit. But, as I've learned, we don't need to put forth effort to get where we want in life; it just happens when we go with the flow.

Can you believe that? We simply put it out there, letting the universe know exactly what we desire and then let it go. We are not meant to suffer, hold on tight and dig our heels in before good things happen to us, like I used to believe. And, it doesn't mean that you have to give up a dream; it just means that you let go of the attachment to your specific desired result.

I understand now that knowing when and how to surrender also takes spiritual maturity. Maybe I was only ready to surrender after I had been through so much hell in my life. How could I surrender anyway when I didn't even trust? How could I surrender when I couldn't let go? I know that we struggle when we don't want to accept what is and we continue to try and make things happen rather than allowing them to unfold. Maybe the universe has something even better in mind for us than what we could have dreamed. When we learn to stop controlling things it ultimately serves our highest good and opens us up to receive; then miracles can happen.

The way to recognize when to surrender is when we have no control over the outcome of a situation. That is when you can stop worrying and understand that whatever happens is for the best for all involved; detach from the outcome, trust and relinquish control to a higher power.

Are you holding onto something tightly because of fear around losing it? Only when you surrender and trust that everything will work out, will it happen.

Looking back I think I began practicing surrender with the little things. I remember dropping a small but beloved earring when I was getting dressed one morning and I could not find it. I had to go to work but didn't forget about it, so, for the next couple of days whenever I had a chance, I kept searching to find it. I was determined that I was not going to give up until I did. Then finally, I got it and told myself to surrender and that maybe I was supposed to learn a lesson from losing it. Within a couple of days, after I had surrendered, something shiny on the floor caught my eye where I hadn't thought to look and there was my earring. I knew my lesson was to practice surrender. I know that if I had continued to hold on to the notion that I would find it, no matter what, then I would be holding on and trying too hard to make things happen and never recover it. Even if the thing you are afraid of losing is small, the feelings attached to it may be deep and need to be felt. Because I let go, a little miracle happened.

Not being able to surrender became clear during Coaching sessions and it was evident that one of the first things I needed to learn was to let go of control. I was meditating daily which was great for me, but I promised myself that I would do it every day at a specific time. That was controlling and I should have been meditating when my spirit called me to; if I miss some days, I miss some days. Colleen also guided me through a meditation more than once that allowed me to recognize my controlling ways and practice letting go and trusting.

Try this exercise to learn to let go and stop controlling:

TRUST AND LET GO

- Find a quiet, comfortable place, lie down and breathe long, slow breaths as you count from 10 down to 1, relaxing more deeply with every count.
- Once you are very calm and relaxed, imagine yourself on a Bridge. Look around and notice the beautiful sky, feel the warmth of the sun and see that the Bridge is a very high one which arches over a river far below.
- Now, stand up on the railing, take a deep breath and jump; yes, jump.
- Feel whatever comes up for you; fear, panic, joy or even anger. Maybe you can't manage to jump the first time you try this exercise. Be okay with whatever you feel and don't judge the process. Just keep practicing until you can do it.
- If you were able to jump, reflect on how you felt doing that and write it down in a journal.
- This is truly what letting go of control feels like as we learn to trust that the universe is always supporting us.

The first time I tried this jumping meditation, I was unable to do it; I had too much fear. After practicing to face my fear, I was able to jump and was surprised after I did, that I could fly. It was so much fun as I floated way above the earth and flew above the treetops; all because I surrendered, trusted and let go of control.

Do you ever find yourself wanting to win an argument or wanting control over someone else in a conversation? The idea that we always have to be right or win puts us in a place of superiority which comes from the ego. We can strengthen our spirit within if we let go of the outcome. When you do, you will notice you have a lot more energy and it's another way of loving yourself.

Decide to stop trying to convince anyone else of anything and you will notice that this helps your control issues. Let others believe what they want to; you don't have to convince them, ever.

I thought I had surrendered when I had to sell my house at a loss. I let go and decided to not worry about the money I owed the bank but looking back, this was easy to do because I was too exhausted and sick to do anything about it anyway. I did not have the energy to be even scared or nervous about not being able to pay the bank the money I owed them so I just let it go and knew I would deal with it later. This worked to my benefit because I needed all my energy to invest in my commitment to heal myself. Some years after, I heard from a collection agency and when they asked me to settle my debt of $33,000, I still was not in a position to pay them. I was however, able to negotiate and settle on an amount that was far less than I had owed them originally. That felt good. I knew I hadn't been irresponsible but rather I was trying to do my best in a difficult situation and sell my house even at a loss so as not to continue to incur any further costs when I couldn't pay my mortgage. After all, I had been sick and was trying hard to make things better. I can see now that being in this position left me feeling shame inside like I was a failure. I was judging myself and trying to control how things would play out in my life.

Throughout the years I was working at the Academy of Design, I continued to collect disability benefits, needing the financial support as I was never quite certain how many classes I was going to teach or how much money I was going to make each term. I was always concerned about not being able to pay my rent and continue to see my practitioners and doctors. Eventually however, I decided that I felt strong enough to give up receiving the CPP monthly payments. This was because I was still healing and knew that while I continued to collect disability, it would have kept me in the energy of being disabled. I knew it was important for me to move forward without it because I was determined to know perfect health and because that took courage to do.

My doctor was very concerned about me giving up the CPP support because she had seen me struggle over so many years and she advised against it. She knew that the disability helped me and did not want to see me relapse under the stress of not being able to pay my medical bills. To move ahead on my own was a challenge but it was important for me to face my fear and trust that the universe was supporting me. Around the same time, after collecting CPP for eight years, the government decided to take a look at my case and felt that the additional income I made had exceeded what was acceptable. They told me I would probably have to pay back what I had received over that time. The government believes that if you can work, you are not disabled but if I hadn't worked, I would never have made the money I needed to improve my health or heal. I followed through with the appropriate paperwork hoping they would recognize that every penny I had earned was for treatments, doctors and therapy and that I had taken responsibility for my own healing.

I felt strongly that I had done everything in my power to heal myself and be able to let go of receiving disability payments but I felt the government might have trouble agreeing with me. After all, it is easier to see when someone is well again when a broken bone heals; it's not the same with chronic fatigue because it is invisible. I see now that it was my soul guiding me along this path that I took and I am thankful that I did have some support and that I could also work sometimes. I could not have done it any other way. Over the years, I had not been vacationing down south, purchasing beautiful clothes or new vehicles nor did I live in a house or condo that I owned. My priority was to be healthy and every ounce of energy went into making that happen. The entire process took about five years to be resolved and during that time I provided the government with everything they needed to make their decision. They finally decided that the entire amount of the disability that I had received over eight years, $42,000 had to be paid back. I appealed this and followed up by sending letters from all my doctors, therapists, practitioners and coaches that I had worked with over the years. We all asked them to reconsider their judgement. All my doctors spoke of my intense desire to heal myself and relayed how they had watched me relapse often and how my quest to be healthy had taken over my life. They all felt that I should not be punished for having to spend so much time and money to get better. Every letter was supportive and clear in its message that I would not be healthy today if I had not taken responsibility and conducted myself with total commitment to be well. I wanted to make sure that I had exhausted every opportunity to have them hear and understand me regarding my experience with chronic fatigue and what it takes to heal it. I knew that others would come along after me with CFS and maybe have to deal with the government in the same situation. Some doctors do not still believe that it is a real disease; they think it is all in your head. I was summoned to a Review Tribunal to discuss my case and eventually they decided that I would pay back the full amount in monthly instalments of $1,000 over five years but how was I going to do that with no savings and no full-time job?

One of my friends hooked me up with a professional who dealt with the government along with the best insolvency lawyer in the city who took on my case for free. He determined that what the government had done to me was completely unacceptable, but that once they decided on something, it was done. He advised me that they were going to get their money, no matter what. I had lived on very little for so long and did not have $1,000 a month to pay them back. Years earlier when I was teaching, I had invested $75,000 in RRSP's that I had held onto tightly; I never considered touching them even when my financial situation was dire. There was no other way that I was going to be able to pay this debt back, so I knew that cashing them would do it and most of my nest egg would be gone.

I had been holding on to this investment tightly because I saw it as my only reserve for the future but now I was determined to cut any ties with the government. I had a desire to rid myself of the old energy that surrounded disability and disease, so, I surrendered. I knew what surrender felt like but this was the most intense I ever experienced and the rush of relief was incredible. It was so freeing and I could not believe how good it felt. What was I holding onto? It was just money; I'd made it before and I'd make it again. I knew now that the universe must have something better in store for me and for my future and I totally trusted that it did. Otherwise, I would not have to be cashing in my RRSP's; everything would work out for me and I was re-confirming my belief in that by letting go and releasing.

I also felt a shift in me that was enormous. Several doors of opportunity opened after that and within a few days, a new boyfriend was on my doorstep. An opportunity to teach in high school also presented itself and both of these things dropped into my life because I was no longer controlling and holding on tightly. Finally, my desire to move back into teaching high school was confirmed and my foot was in the door. I made the transition from teaching college during the day to teaching evenings and teaching high school for five weeks as I took over for someone finishing up maternity leave. I also still sold furniture on the weekends.

So, now that I knew how to really surrender, the universe showed me it was going to give me other opportunities to practice. This was clear when I received notice from the Canada Revenue Agency that they decided to audit my small business. I followed instructions, and sent in the documents. They were straightforward in their expectation of me paying them back the $16,000 which they felt I owed them and they wanted it immediately. This was the balance of what was left of my RRSP's so I just cashed in everything, wrote them a cheque for that amount and decided to move on with my life. I thought I was poor before; but now, I was really broke. That was okay because I knew what that felt like. I knew that if I was living in the present, it didn't matter because I had enough right now. I felt free and I felt strong and empowered because of all of it.

I started supply teaching regularly for the Peel Board of Education and also did Long Term Occasional work. Because I wanted to use the skills I had learned as a working artist, designer and entrepreneur, I had my heart set on teaching art again and wanted a full time contract. I did apply for art jobs that came along at year end, but, they were rare at best and were usually filled internally. For the next couple of years I was seeing the signs that there was no movement in art, so I decided to re-brand myself and go in a new direction teaching entrepreneurship and business courses. I knew that special education was a growing field also, was very drawn to that student and so I took some additional qualification courses to enable me to teach in several new subject areas; I surrendered. I felt like the notion that I was returning to teach art was no longer viable and my soul was showing me a new path to walk, yet again. I was just fine surrendering to this idea because at this point, I was hearing the guidance clearer than ever before. I needed a full-time contract teaching so whatever my soul guided me to teach was fine with me. Surrendering was becoming easier and easier. Once you hear and see the signs, it's simple to follow them.

To help attract a full time opportunity into my life, I put myself in the energy of being a full time staff member where I was supply teaching. I behaved like it was happening already. Because I was a supply teacher, I had more spare time to do creative work and have a hand in helping improve the school's climate for learning by being on committees and showing up every day as if it was my full time job. Sometimes my colleagues would ask me why I thought I had not yet been able to sign a permanent contract and I would always say that it just wasn't time yet; it would happen.

Sometimes things don't happen as quickly as we would like because we have to learn patience. And, sometimes things don't happen when we would like them to so that it brings up emotions like frustration or fear so we can heal them.

I just kept moving forward, believing that I would land a position and after five years, I did. I applied to be a full time art teacher at The Roy McMurtry Youth Centre which is a secure facility teaching incarcerated youth. Because I had surrendered and trusted that everything would work out and I was no longer holding on tightly to the notion of only teaching art, an art position presented itself. I had taken all the pressure off myself by letting go of control and believing that if I did not get that job then something even better would be down the road for me, and a miracle happened.

I had learned to go with the flow and will always remember how ecstatic I was to receive the phone call offering me the contract. And, it is the best job I have ever had in my life; my students are the most remarkable, amazing and interesting people I have ever had the pleasure to teach. My colleagues also show me that this very special teaching experience attracts only very special people. I feel fulfilled which was something I longed for and I know that I am doing what I am meant to do. I had come full circle and returned back to teach and do things differently this time with all the experience, wisdom and knowledge I had gained over the years when I was healing myself and it feels good to have learned so much.

Practice this exercise on visualizing a goal but letting go of control to help make it happen.

SURRENDER

- Think of a goal you would like to achieve. This could be a new job, a relationship, a new place to live or anything you would like to see happen in your life.
- Sit or lie down in a comfortable place, breathe deeply and slowly, relaxing your body completely.
- Count down from 10 to 1, going deeper and deeper into at state of peace and relaxation with each count.
- Imagine the thing you want and picture yourself enjoying it, experiencing it, playing with it if it's an object, and being there feeling all the positive, loving emotions that would be involved if it was happening now. See it, smell it and feel it as if in a daydream to make it more real.
- You can do this for any amount of time which feels good to you but practice keeping that energy alive to attract this desire into your life. Say positive affirmations as if it were happening right now including, 'for the highest good of all concerned.'
- Now let it go. Surrender to whatever happens knowing that the universe may have something in mind for you that may be even better than you could have imagined yourself.
- Practice this exercise daily and trust, surrender letting it go and just believe.

Throughout my life, I always tried so hard at everything but now I know I don't have to try at all. Once, I believed that things were difficult, but now, I see that I am supported by an abundant universe and I am never alone. I have learned to ask clearly for what I want but then detach from the outcome and be aware of any signs that come along that may end up showing me a new direction to move in.

Things do unfold as they should and it is not necessary to squeeze them out of the universe like I once tried to do using the strong, male energy that drove me. I was working against myself. People often ask me at New Year's if I have a resolution for the year. I used to be so driven to accomplish my goals in life that I would control, hold on tight, be determined and strive to make them happen. So, now I respond by saying that I stopped making resolutions and instead, I watch for the signs that guide me to the goals my soul knows I need to accomplish, and I surrender.

Everything unfolds gently on its own time without me having to try and make it happen. Life is much more peaceful for me these days.

SURRENDER AND LET GO

- Meditate daily and ask for help to let go of control.
- Admit that you have no control over what happens and take responsibility for this.
- Think of a situation in your life that you really have no control over the outcome of and have probably been concerned about.
- Hand it over; let go and let God.
- You will feel lighter as you have given away your tension and stress; you will notice your health improve and you'll sleep better at night.

10. intention

Our intention creates our reality.

-Wayne Dyer

Intention is a powerful thing. With the desire to achieve something which is for our highest good, our intention will attract the universe's energy and it will happen.

Looking back, I see that my determination and desire were a part of the intention I maintained to heal my body. I also wanted to resurrect my soul, find the source of my illness and get over my fear around money; these goals all came to fruition for me. I see now that the universe conspired with me to make everything happen because of my intention. The universe even helped create a new direction for me to go and a desire in me to want to teach in high school again after so many years of being absolutely positive that I would never go back to that old career.

My intention and curiosity to find the source of this ill health that I suffered had never wavered. After becoming a Life Coach and

Hypnotherapist, I was able to work with a medical intuitive who came to Ontario once a month from Florida. A group of us who are spiritually involved and interested in deep healing and doing soul work had the opportunity to benefit from her treatments both when she was here and also long distance from Sarasota.

She was able to tap into my energy and understand what was going on in my body and my consciousness even when she was far away. When she was working with her guides, she uncovered the truth that I had been born healthy but a few months into my life, I had been afflicted by some trauma which left me with a broken immune system that let in three viruses. One virus had been hiding in my lymphatic system so no one was ever able to find and diagnose it. After hearing that truth, I sensed intuitively that the trauma was a loud noise of some kind that shocked and frightened me as a baby and was something my parents would not have ever imagined would have such an impact on me for my entire life. My consciousness left my body in that noisy shock and the trauma left me distressed. It was important for me to know this and I felt relieved to see that the illness I suffered was in this present lifetime although also affected by my past lives.

Think of an aim and affirm it by speaking out loud stating your intention. Once this is done, stay sharp and be aware and willing to receive any guidance that comes your way that connects you to your source and your intention will be sealed.

Although I have come a great distance in my life, I intend to continue on my path to further and deeper healing and I receive confirmation through my experiences, which prove that I am supported in this aim. While writing the initial draft of this book, I felt every day like I was fighting my way through a very bad snowstorm. It was difficult for me to go back and feel the pain of the memories of everything I had been through. To crawl back into that darkness that I had worked so hard to escape from was an arduous task but I knew it would be healing. And what made it worse was, as I wrote telling my stories I began to also re-live some of the old symptoms. Somehow, I knew that writing would be a positive experience but once I started having symptoms that I had not experienced in many years, I knew that I was healing the crumbs of what was left over from that old lack of ease in my body. The memories that I wrote about were bringing anything left over from my unhealthy self back to the surface to be dealt with.

My apartment felt exceedingly cold; I kept going to the radiators and checking whether they were on and working. It felt to me like the heat was off completely. I knew that it was the memory of the Concentration Camp and working hard labour during the winter where we froze. We worked outside with bare feet and had no outerwear. Recurrences of cold sores, Raynaud's Syndrome and spontaneous viruses in my computer were all appearing again and reflecting my past.

I knew they were a gift, taking me deeper as my health and the health of my computer were mirrors of my old illness. The ring that I have never taken off in twenty years started to burn my finger again. After my mother's death, my father had passed her engagement ring on to me and I designed a new one, changed the setting while using the diamonds. I love my ring and although it is 14 -karat gold, when I was unhealthy many years ago, it would periodically react and burn my finger, causing blisters and a lot of discomfort. I always thought it was because my body was toxic, the metal reacted to me but it would come and go with no connection to any reason why so I was always confused by it. My family doctor said I was having an allergic reaction but I didn't buy this because most of the time it was just fine. I always knew it was something I would figure out and I was curious and intent upon healing it.

Since, at this point, I had been very healthy and the ring had not reacted to my body in many years, I was interested in this onset of this pain again and why this time it returned with a vengeance. I knew that the issue had resurfaced so that I could get to the source of it and that it was a sign. I was now spiritually mature enough to face why it was burning me and just like the noise in my apartment stopped once I knew about my death as a Viking, I knew this too would stop happening. This time though, the reaction was more severe and constant than ever before. I needed to give my finger a rest to heal but was concerned about removing the ring and leaving it at home. All the little tricks I once used to employ and separate my finger from the ring using tape or nail polish didn't work this time. The pain and discomfort persisted and were the call from my soul to return to that deeper part of me where the truth had been hiding and where I needed to go to in order to heal that wound; but, what was it? Only then would I be able to wear my ring again. This reaffirmed my intention to find out why this was happening.

Determined to heal, I went into my memories; something that is easy for me to do now with self-hypnosis. I thought it might have been related to the many times I had been tortured and murdered in past lives for being a witch, a psychic and a seer. In fact I had denied and dismissed my psychic, intuitive gifts in this lifetime for so long because of the fear of these past traumatic events.

Doing this work brought up several separate occurrences from past lives when I had been persecuted for being a psychic. In one lifetime, it was 1710 and at my death scene I saw myself standing on sticks that were set ablaze, the way Joan of Arc had died. In another, I was a man in the 1600's and I saw myself running away from people who were chasing me for helping others with my intuitive powers. I saw a sword pierce my heart as they captured and murdered me because of their fear and lack of understanding of my clairvoyance. Of course, back then they thought we were witches and I died painful, horrific deaths and brought this trauma and fear into my present life, always denying even to myself that I had intuitive abilities that could help others.

In my third past life, I saw myself as a man of the clergy, dressed in black; I see my black boots as I am tied to a gurney or frame work and am tortured in water, suffering as I slowly drown. It was the other members of the clergy that were afraid of me and my abilities so there was also the sense of betrayal along with dying this way that has haunted me even in this lifetime. In fact, water and swimming have never been among my favourite things and this explains why. I thought that the fires which had burned me when I died may also be burning my ring into my flesh and left this memory branded into my soul. But after I visited these scenes several times, I was convinced that these three lifetimes did not hold the key to why my ring was burning me. Internationally renowned author Louise Hay would say that that the ring finger symbolizes grief so I naturally again, went to the loss of my little boy in the Concentration Camps to feel that pain, hoping it was the source of my hurt.

What was it that was trying to get my attention? Was my little boy connected to the symbol of grief in my ring or was it something else in the Camps? My intent to find out along with my angel's guidance led me to ask my hypnotist friend to facilitate some healing through a past life regression.

When regressed, I found myself again in the Camps. I have been there so often before and did not have to go deep to feel familiar and connected to that place. I saw me standing with an old dress on, bare feet and looking extremely sad. My ring finger was dripping blood and I wondered about that as well as my bare feet until I read that this is how they dressed us in the Ravensbrück Concentration Camp during the war. There was a Nazi guard in uniform who materialized behind me but there was softness about him, not threatening or dark in his energy but doing his job as a Nazi; he was not a bully. This was interesting and I wondered why there would be a man beside me who was so gentle and nonviolent in that place. It later came to me that I had been involved with him in the Camps and he had kept me alive for a while. However forbidden, we loved each other passionately and deeply and of course, it was a secret. I only recently understand that I had never detached from him and that trauma of losing this secret love. I continue to heal this relationship by remembering, feeling and detaching from him now, unable to move forward until I do.

The week after my regression, it was no coincidence that John of God – or João de Deus, the Brazilian spiritual healer – was coming to Toronto and I felt blessed when I knew I could see him for help healing this deep past life trauma. John of God's ability to perform psychic surgeries on people with the help of his entities allows us to heal both physically and emotionally and we transform spiritually because of it. The fact that I was still unable to put my ring on and wear it without it blistering and burning my finger was a clear sign that I was not getting to the source of my pain and grief and I needed his help to go deeper. I understood that the wound would never go away, but I knew it could be healed once I got to its origin. John of God requested that everyone wear white and as I arrived that day at the Convention Centre, I was taken away by the vibration because the energy was so high. I felt lifted by it as the sheer bliss in the building was so elevated that it transported me away every second that I did not have to be in my conscious mind thinking and conversing with people around me. It was heaven to be there so easily transported into the ethers.

That day John of God decided he would perform a psychic surgery on everyone so we stood in line and prepared ourselves to go before him and have an intervention. Part of our healing included instructions to follow for 40 days and prescription water to drink daily to keep the vibration of the entities alive as they continued to work on us. I wondered if I would be able to sleep for 12 hours, not watch television or use a computer or a telephone until the next day – all part of our instructions. But, I did feel groggy from the spiritual anaesthetic and had no problems sleeping it off as I detoxified its effects. I could feel where the incision had been made in my body by the entities and that week I was able to wear my ring again although I felt the healing continuing. My desire was still strong to find the source of why I saw that finger dripping blood when I was in hypnosis and the details of why my ring continued to get my attention by burning me.

It was important for me to know the truth of this past life trauma and I knew that if I continued to ask my angels and my soul for help, they would send it. I explained that I needed their guidance so I could see where this ring issue was coming from and that they could send it to me in a dream or any other way they wanted to. I knew they would respond so I let it go and forgot about it. Later that week, in the middle of the night, I suddenly woke up in a panic. I was feeling the kind of overwhelming fear that someone feels if they are claustrophobic; no amount of soothing was going to settle me down although I tried. The feeling that I was close to death was clear and I knew it was real. 'I have to get my ring off, I can't get my ring off, I have to get my ring off, I can't get my ring off ', is what kept running through my mind.

I knew this was a sign and that I had to feel this memory but it was intense and the sense of being very close to death left me terrorized. I got out of bed and walked around my bedroom trying to calm myself by breathing slowly. 'You're here now so just breathe, you are okay,' I repeated over and over to myself. I had an overwhelming feeling that my ring was too tight and I couldn't get it off but when I checked, I was able to move it on my finger and there was play there. This however, did not stop my intense anxiety, 'I have to get it off; I have to get it off!'

I walked into my kitchen and felt my mother speak to me saying, 'Use butter,' so I went to the refrigerator and got butter to grease my finger and proceeded to try to remove it through my panic and desperation. I just knew that I would never put it back on again once it was off. I got the ring to my knuckle where it stayed and no amount of pulling or twisting would move it off my finger which made me cry and panic even more so. As I struggled and wept, I suddenly saw a vision of the Concentration Camps and saw me being forced by a guard to remove my wedding ring which he wanted for himself. He followed me around, determined to bully me into giving him my ring and when I continued to refuse, he decided to cut my finger off to get it. I felt the panic of his threat and the resulting powerful desire to remove my ring before he could cut off my finger with his knife. He didn't care about my finger or my welfare or anything; he was a Nazi and he wanted my ring for himself and he was going to get it.

After seeing and feeling this vision while struggling in my kitchen, the ring came off. That was it. I had the answer that I had asked my angels and my soul to help me find out. Once again, the Concentration Camps were the source of this pain and now I would heal it. That memory of being forced to take off my wedding ring and the fear of not being able to, once again created such anxiety that it left a stain on my soul. To the Nazis, it was just one more small fragment of gold to add to their coffers. In the Camps people facing death often buried their precious items to keep them from going to the Nazis, as a final act of defiance.

Now, I wear my ring and it hasn't bothered me since then. I am hoping that it is healed but one never really knows. All we can do it keep showing up for ourselves and feeling the emotions that allow us to heal these deep wounds and I will continue to do just that; it really is great work.

A ring is a symbol of love and we understand this when we exchange engagement and weddings rings. I know now that my ring showed up as a symbol to communicate that I had learned to love myself and once I felt deserving, I would know the truth. I see that everything I have been through with my healing has happened so I can guide and help others also heal their bodies, their hearts and their souls as well; everything I have experienced is a gift.

I recognize daily the way that others create illness within themselves because they are either unaware that they could improve their lives by doing work on their self-worth or their lack of self-love prevents them from consciously understanding that they can change things by this method. Our words are powerful and when we change the way we speak, we can change our lives.

Illness is often complicated and multi-factorial in its origin but we always create it ourselves. It's not something that just happens to us but rather we invite sickness into our bodies. Positive thoughts and words are what we need to have instead of negative ones that are sickening and causing us illness. When we stop complaining about being sick or blaming others when we catch something from them, we will change our lives and be healthy. We invite their illness in because of our negative beliefs.

We need to look deeper inside ourselves and be truthful about our intentions and recognize that we have an inner need for attention or sympathy when we make ourselves sick. I see all the time how people create illness to feed their own neediness as I once did. We get sick as a response to some negative, inner, unconscious belief system, which we can change. It comes from our subconscious and embodies a desire to find an answer to some problem we think we have.

We can transform our lives by changing the way we think and what we think and talk about. Will Bowen's *A Complaint Free World*, (Doubleday 2007) has been one of the most powerful books I have ever experienced reading and will change anyone's life who is ready to take responsibility for their own happiness.

Will told his congregation that he wanted to stop complaining and encouraged them to also take up the challenge. Less than a year after that, more than 6 million people had decided to stop criticizing, gossiping and complaining and have taken on a new, positive habit instead. They have affected change that has eradicated illness and inspired others around the world to do so as well.

A COMPLAINT FREE DAY

- Challenge yourself for one day to say only positive things. Put forth the intention to do this and ask your angels to help you notice before you speak if you are about to say something negative, critical or complaining.
- If you find yourself saying something negative, then stop and reframe it by changing it into something positive in your words and its energy.
- Notice how you feel while doing this and how you feel at the end of the day by eradicating negative talk from your life.
- Consider living a Complaint Free Life by taking on the challenge presented in Will Bowen's book. It only takes three weeks to change a habit but however long it takes, know that you will be a different, healthier, happier person when you accomplish your goal to stop complaining and you will inspire others.

Often people feel guilty about taking time off work so they create illness in order to stay home. Sometimes our self-worth is low and we need to relax but only allow ourselves to do so if we are sick. Some of us use negative words to describe ourselves and say things like, 'I get sick with a cold every October.' Our words are so powerful that people don't realize that they are getting sick every October because they are telling themselves to do so and then they accept the inevitability of it.

When we make ourselves sick, we are feeding something in our emotional body that makes us feel better. So many people don't realize their power and awesomeness so they create a block inside themselves to hold themselves back from achieving their inherent greatness. What we believe, results in our body expressing this through illness. Our fear holds us back; our lack of self-worth holds us back. This I know from experience.

The next time you get sick with anything, take a look at the underlying truth of what is feeding you about this illness. Be honest about your intentions even if they are unconscious because you are getting some kind of payback from being ill. When you take responsibility and love yourself, your body will follow and be healthy.

As a child with eight siblings, I know now that I didn't feel my parent's love. Although they did the best they could, I felt that they did not have time for me and later in life I can remember feeling loved when I went into the hospital for a day or two for some small procedure. It struck me then that I felt taken care of, loved, nurtured and that I mattered to the nurses that constantly came into my room checking up on me; it felt good. I had never had that feeling before and I felt so safe in that place. But I also felt sad that it had to be in the hospital and in this way that I felt loved.

We even have the power to create cancer and often, we can heal it too if we can get to the emotional source of it. I have witnessed this more than once. People have also healed themselves of very serious, chronic illnesses when they have decided to forgive others and they clear out the old stored up anger, resentment and hostility inside themselves. Forgiving others creates a release and is also very healing.

FORGIVENESS HEALS

- Think of someone in your life that you have hurt or treated unfairly.
- Close your eyes, breathe deeply and slowly relax yourself imagining them in front of you as you explain how you hurt them and ask for their forgiveness. Picture them blessing you with their forgiveness and hear their words and feel their love.
- Now, forgive yourself for anything that you feel you should have done better. Then let it go.
- Extend the feeling of forgiveness by writing a list of everyone you have mistreated in some way and follow the same exercise for them making sure to forgive you also. Both your energy and the energy of the other person will be altered by doing this exercise and you will feel the difference afterwards.

When we learn to recognize our own power and change our belief systems and aim for positivity in our words and thoughts, our bodies will reflect a happy, healthy state. After all, our bodies want to be healthy and always are working to find their way back to perfect health which is their natural condition.

We need to help our body do this by aligning our consciousness with our highest spiritual recognition and the physical will follow. Know that it's not a bad thing when we are sick physically and we need to look at it as a gift because there is a message being communicated from within. We can take our own healing into our own hands once we see the belief system that misguides us, acknowledge it and change it by taking responsibility. When we are honest, authentic and change our beliefs we can heal ourselves.

I have not missed a day of work or even had the flu or a cold in more than fifteen years. I work seven days a week most of the time and I have many jobs. I sometimes feel my body beginning to show me something and intuitively feel my immune system calling out from my subconscious that it is being challenged. When this happens, I listen, draw my energy in, boost my immune system, take care of myself and love myself a little more than I have been. It is a message reminding me to slow down or relax more and it always comes back to my self-worth. As a result of doing this no illness has manifested itself in my body. I am a healer and it feels empowering to know that I have healed myself through my intention and hard work to do so.

In our humanness we are perfect and need to learn to accept and love everything about ourselves. No one needs to be fixed. We are awesome just the way we are. We can decide to make changes though, take responsibility, love ourselves, be authentic and heal our past to live a happy, healthy life.

You can do it too; just like I did.

Nancy Newman

you can do it too!